THIS BOOK

BELONGS

TO

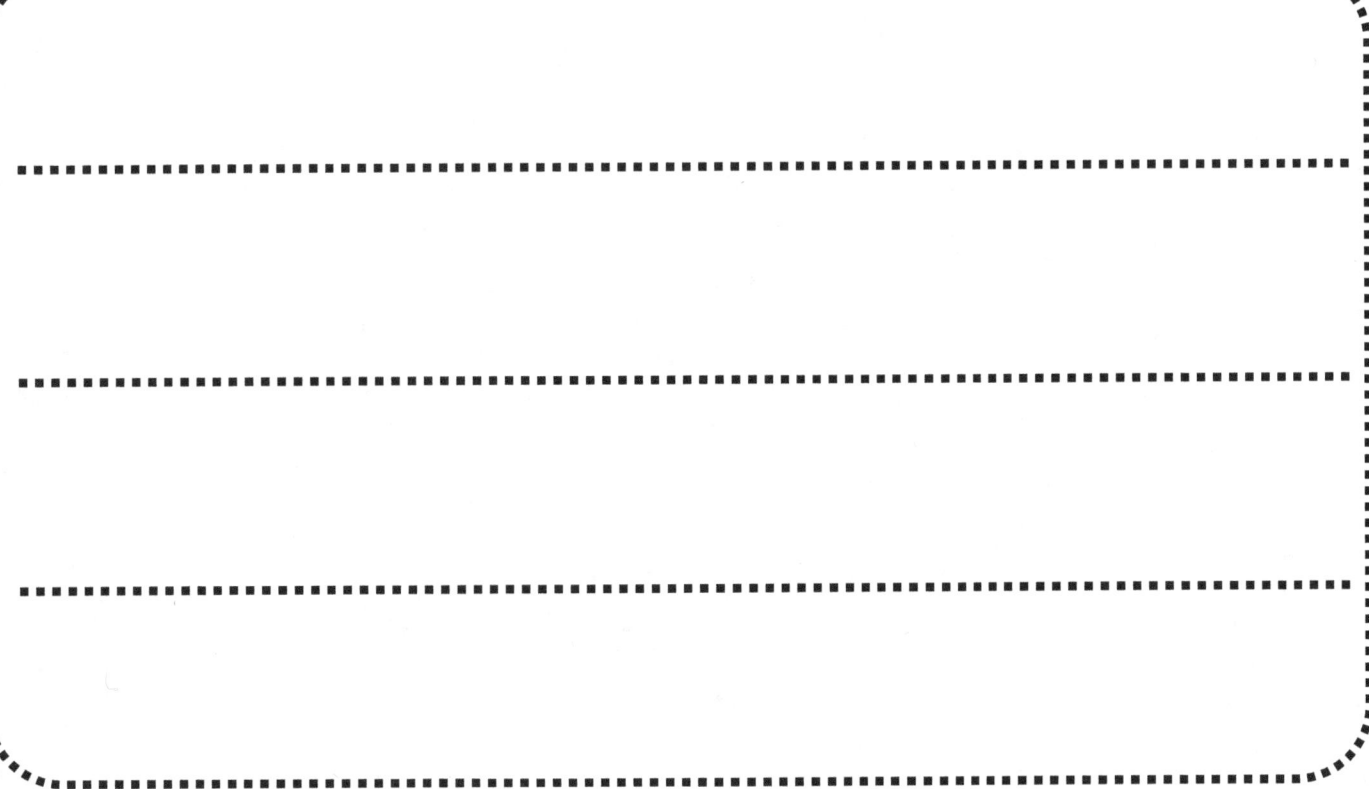

How to use this book

Using our adult coloring book for relaxation and stress relief is simple and rewarding. Follow these steps to unlock its full potential:

Find a Quiet Space: Choose a peaceful environment where you can fully immerse yourself in the coloring experience. Create a cozy nook with soft lighting and comfortable seating to enhance relaxation.

Set the Mood: Play soothing music or light scented candles to enhance the calming ambiance. Take a few deep breaths to center yourself and let go of any tension or stress.

Select Your Coloring Tools: Choose your favorite coloring tools, whether it's colored pencils, markers, or crayons. Experiment with different textures and colors to unleash your creativity.

Explore the Pages: Browse through the pages of the coloring book and choose a design that resonates with you. Trust your intuition and select a drawing that captures your interest and sparks your imagination.

Dive In: Begin coloring with a gentle touch, allowing the colors to flow naturally onto the page. Focus on the present moment and let go of any distractions or worries. Allow yourself to get lost in the creative process and enjoy the meditative rhythm of coloring.

Take Breaks: Remember to take breaks as needed to stretch, hydrate, and rest your eyes. Use this time to reflect on your progress and appreciate the beauty of your work.

Embrace Imperfection: Don't worry about making mistakes or staying within the lines. Embrace imperfection as part of the creative journey and let go of perfectionism. Allow yourself to express freely and enjoy the freedom of self-expression.

Reflect and Relax: After completing a coloring session, take a moment to reflect on how you feel. Notice any changes in your mood, stress levels, or overall well-being. Allow yourself to bask in the sense of accomplishment and relaxation that coloring brings.

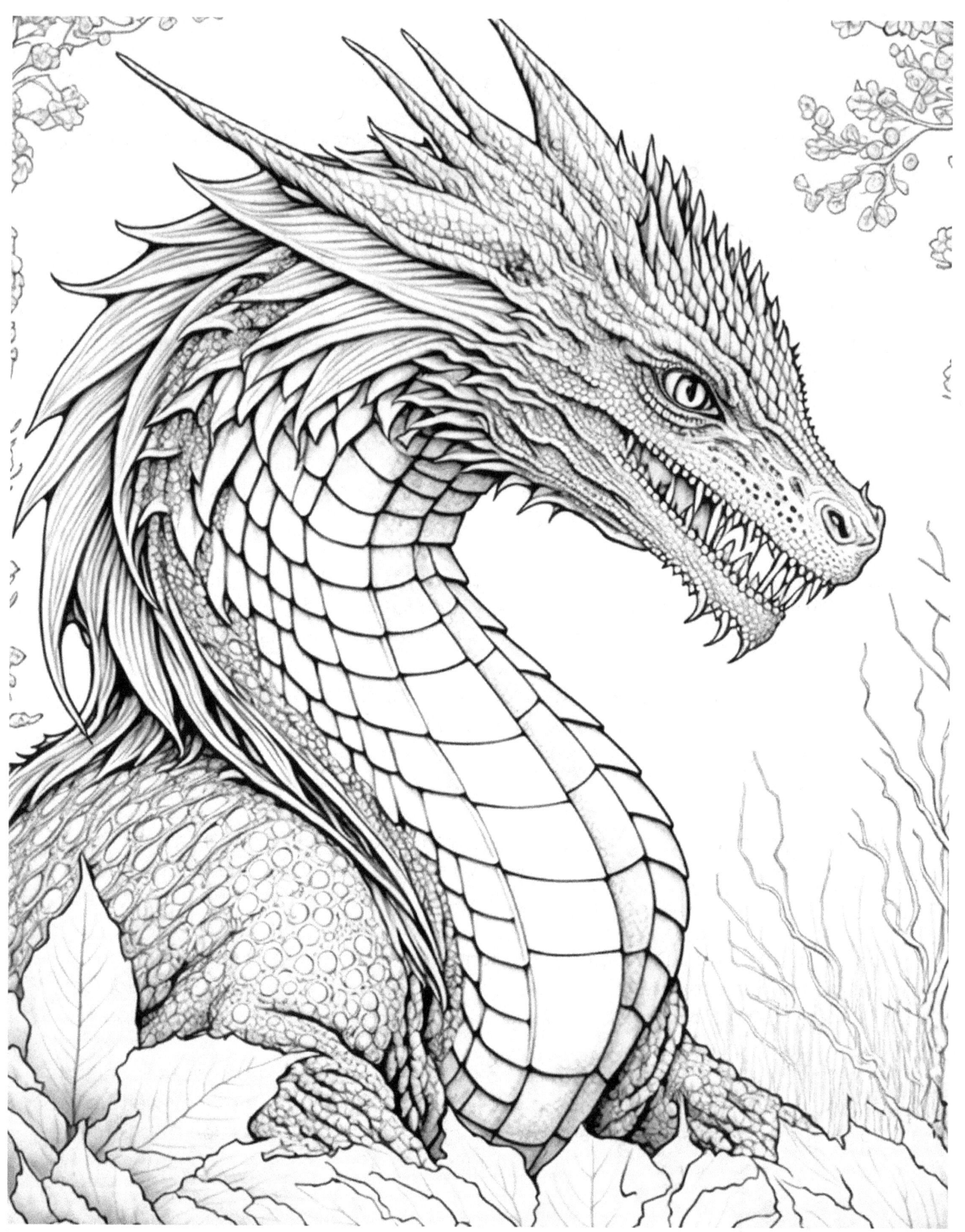

SPYING DRAGONS

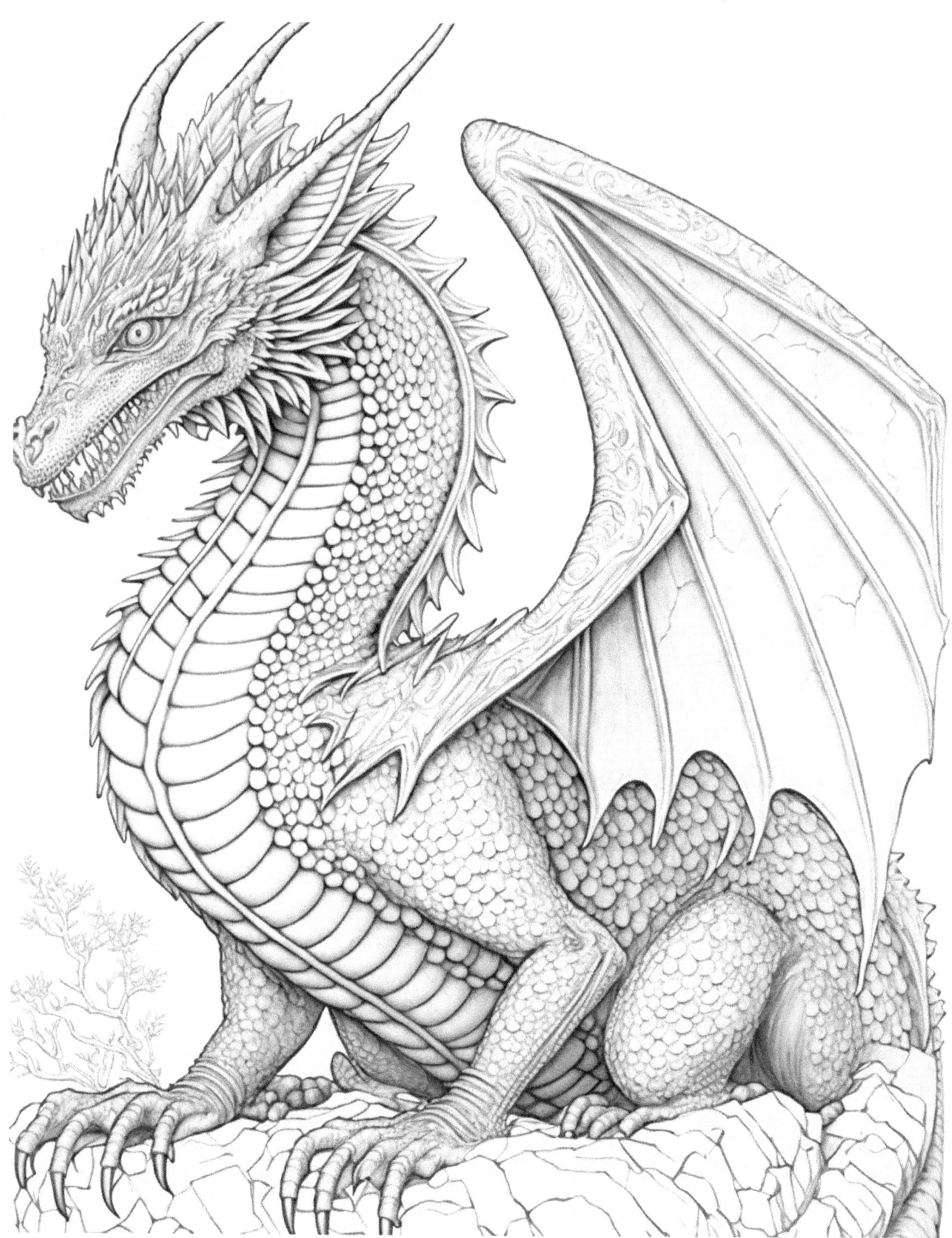

SPYING DRAGONS

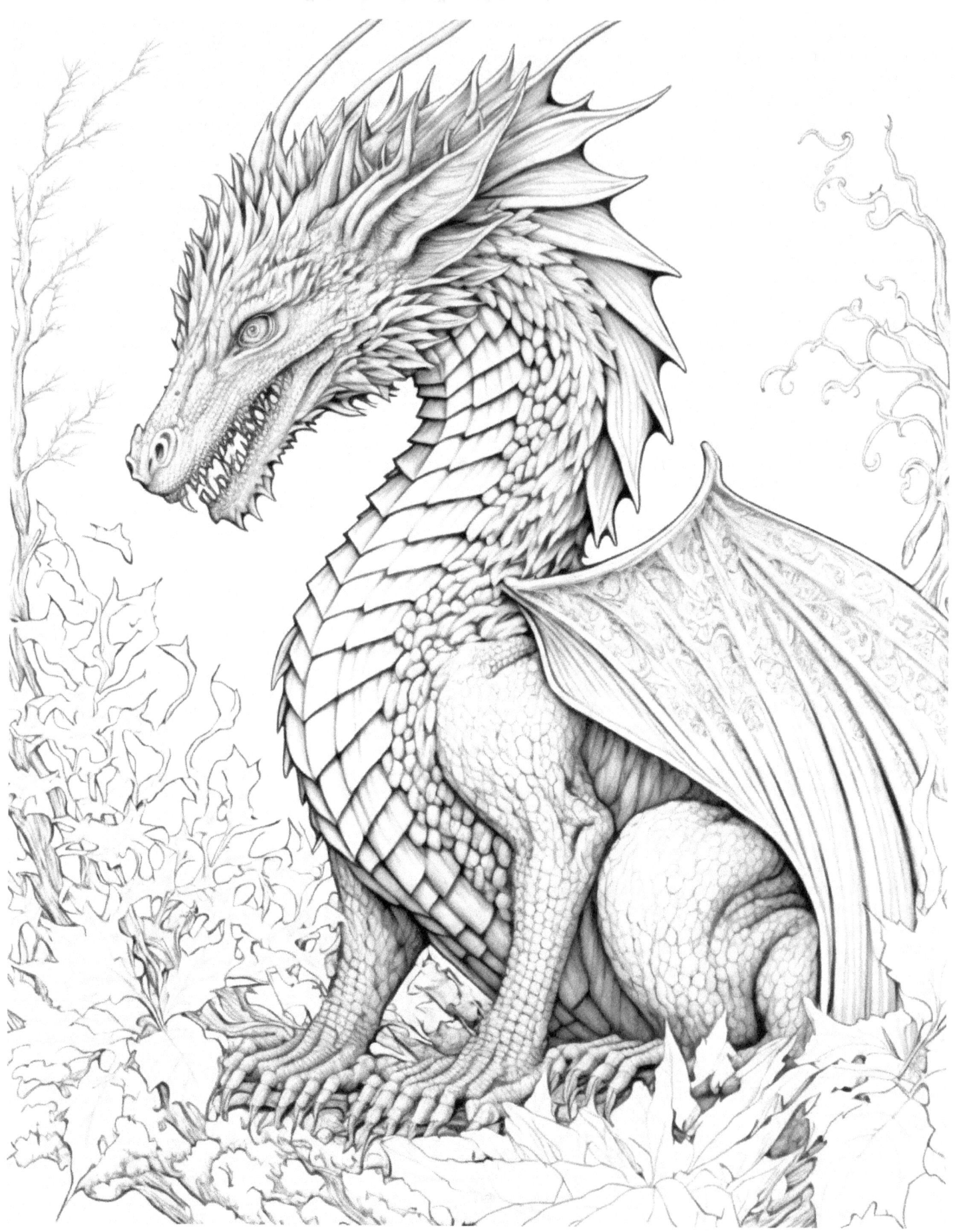

SPYING DRAGONS

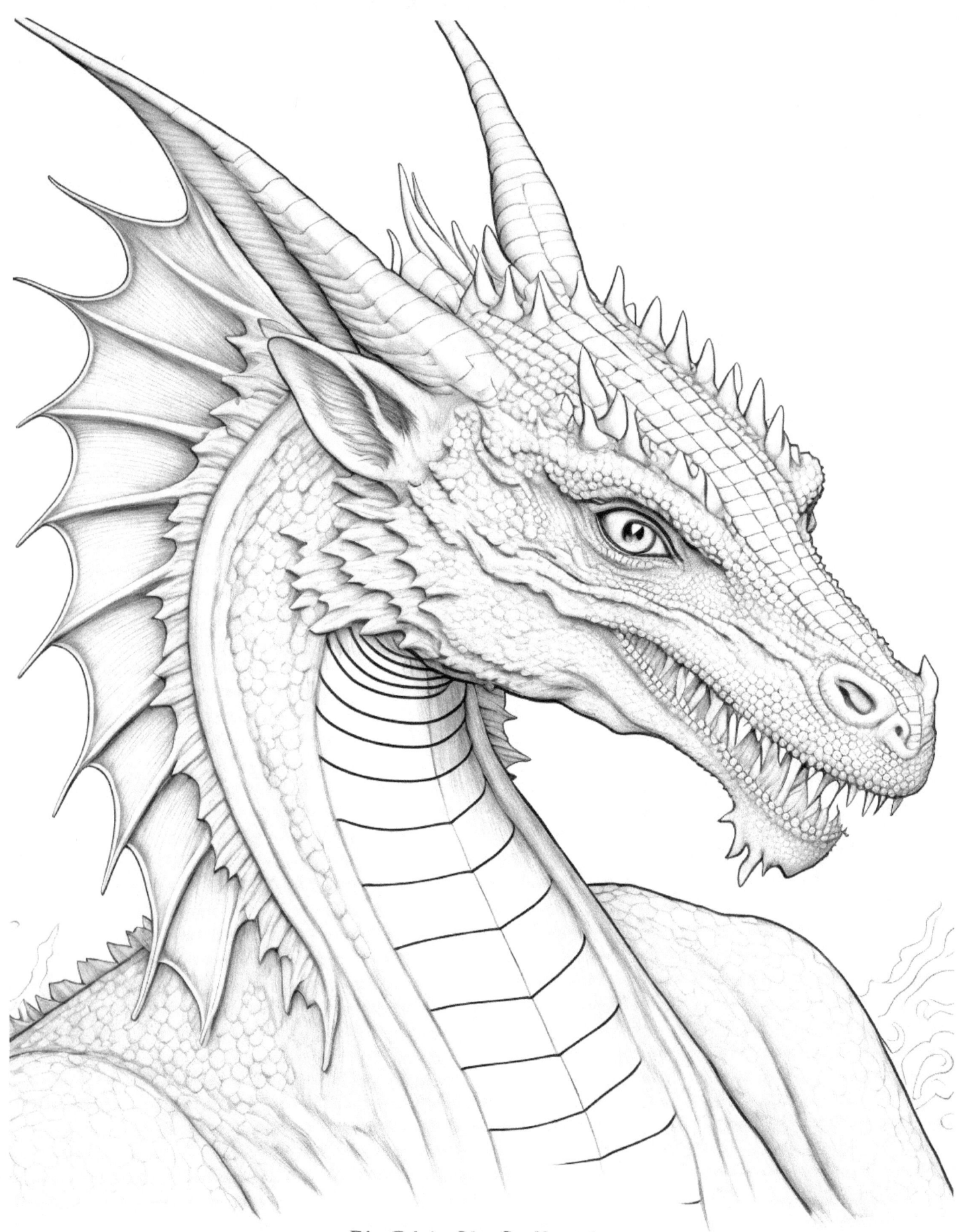

SPYING DRAGONS

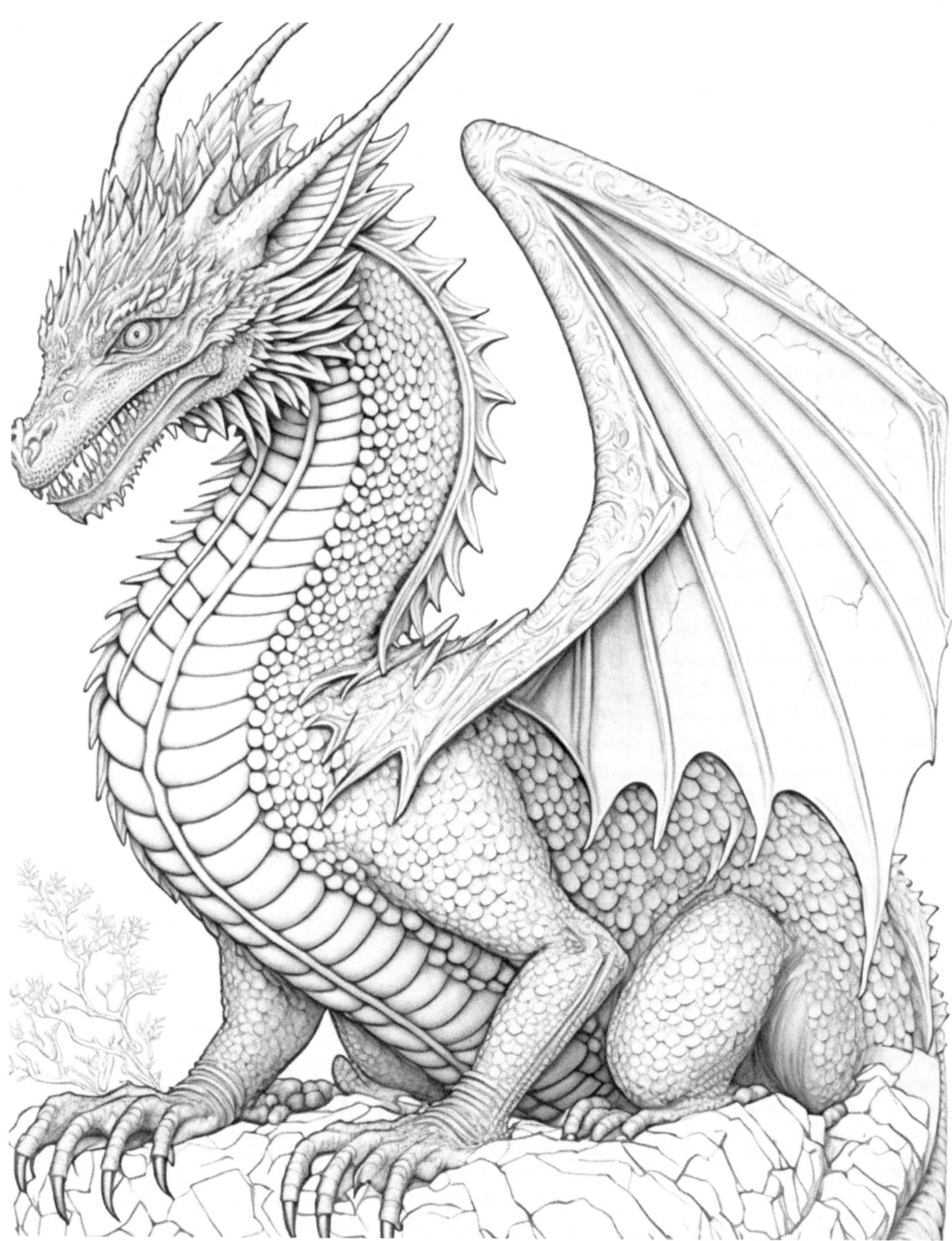

SPYING DRAGONS

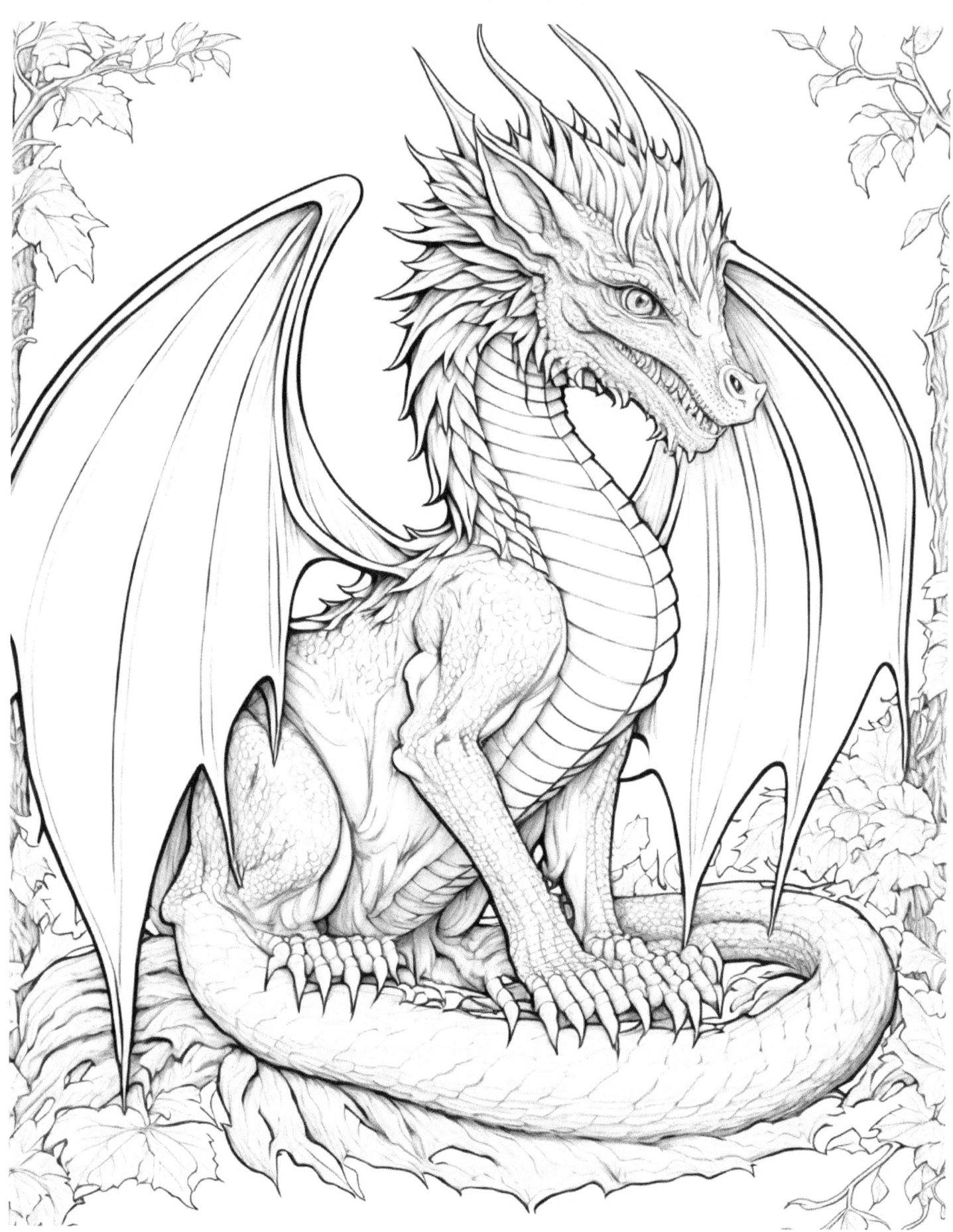

SPYING DRAGONS

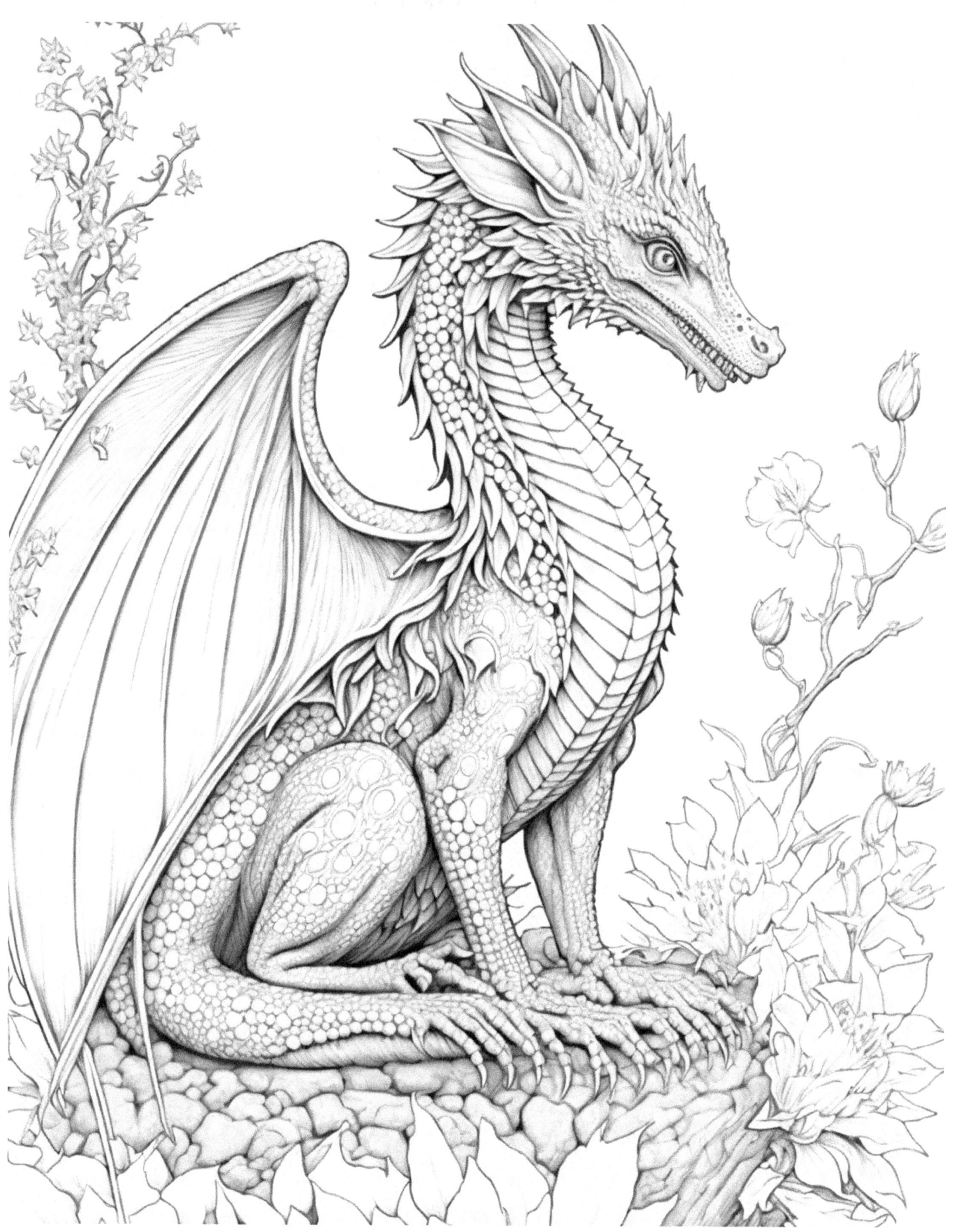

SPYING DRAGONS

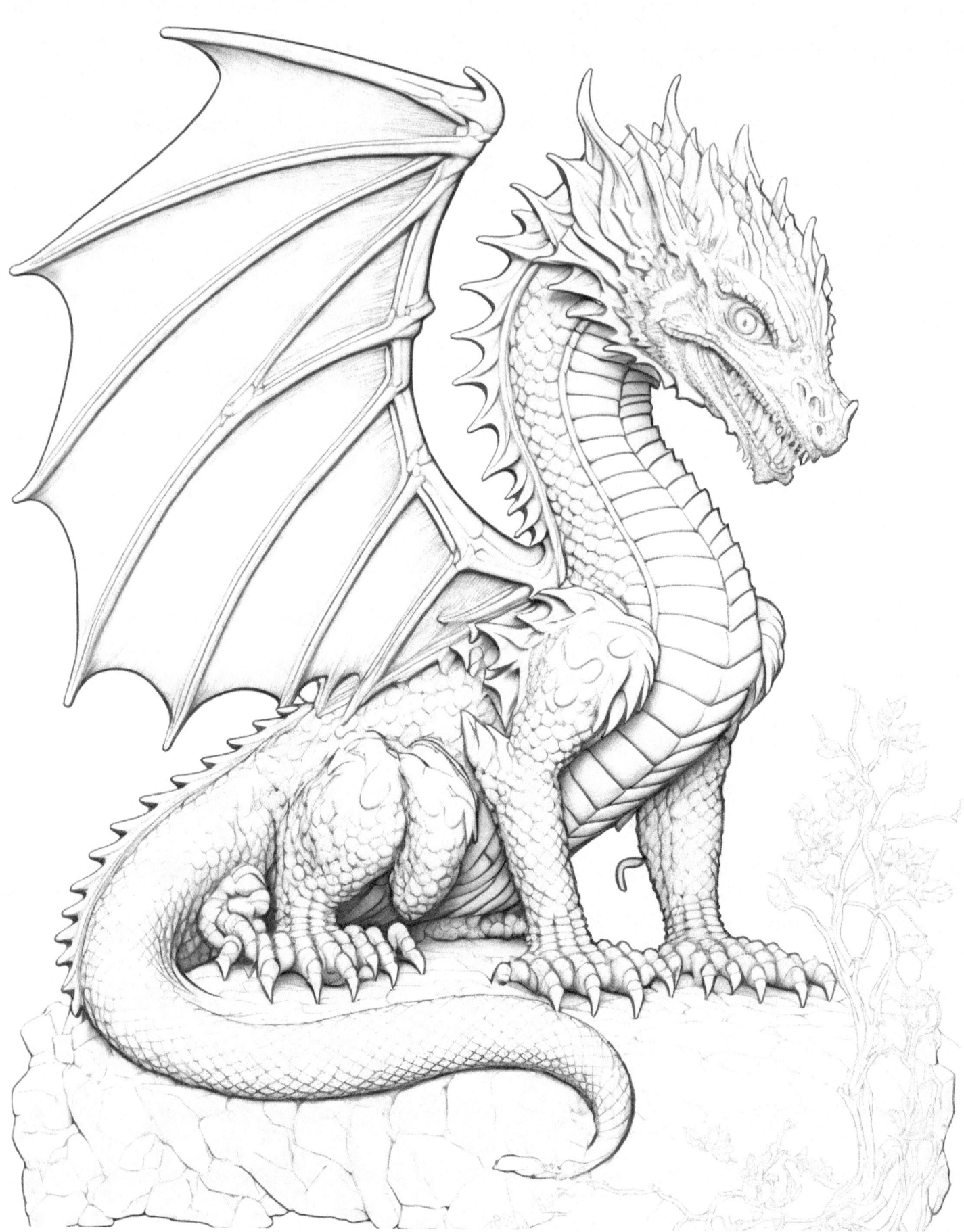

SPYING DRAGONS

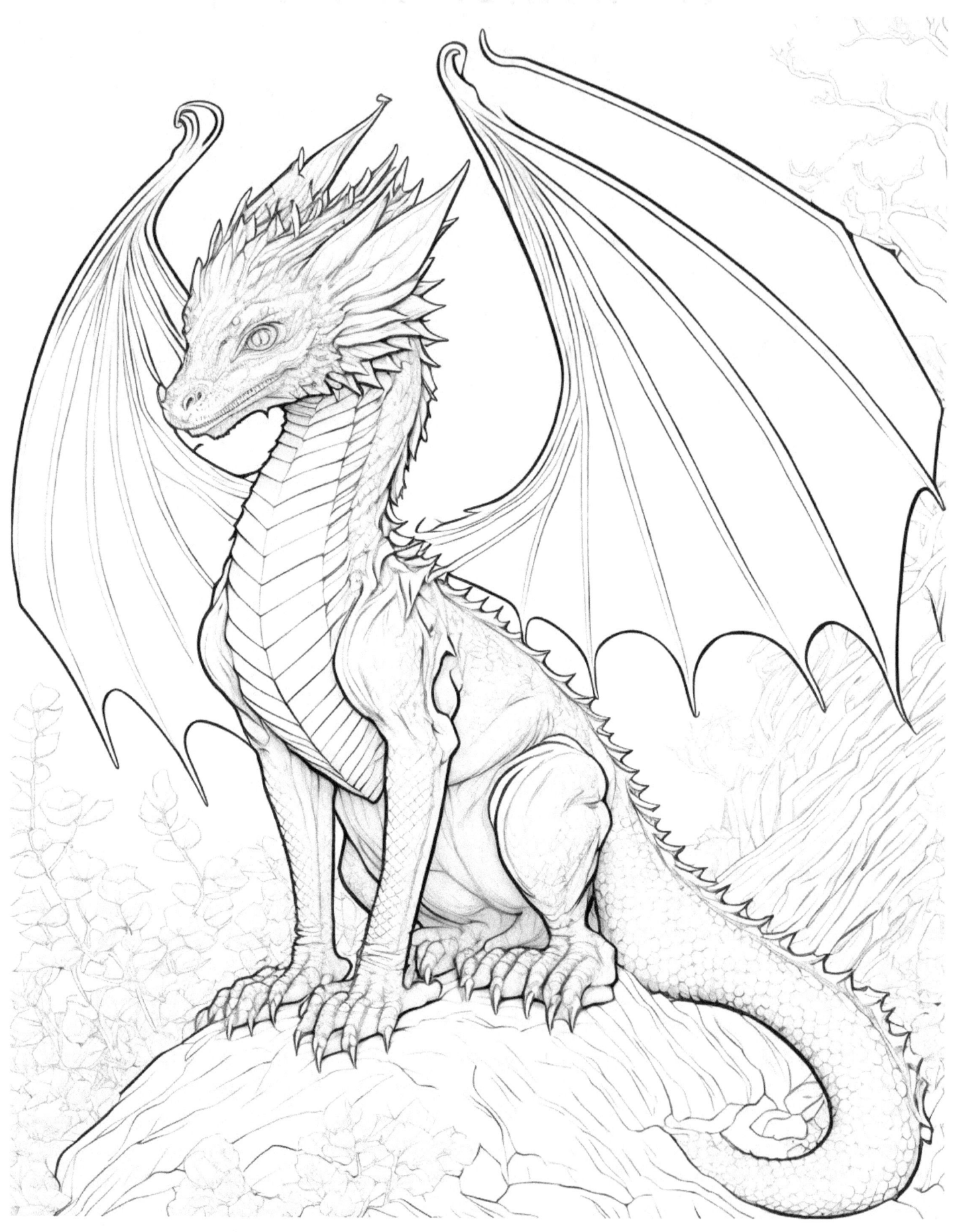

SPYING DRAGONS

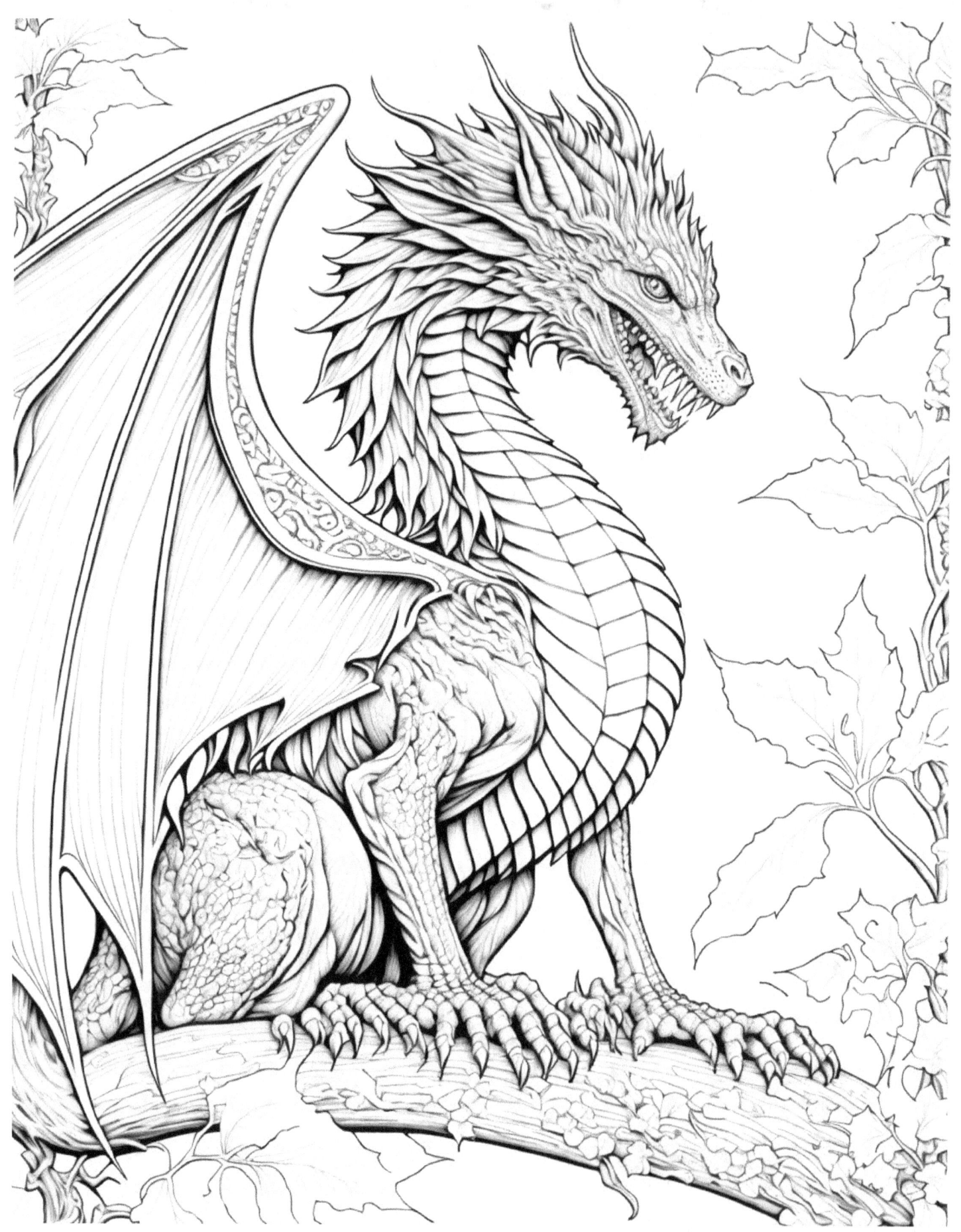

SPYING DRAGONS

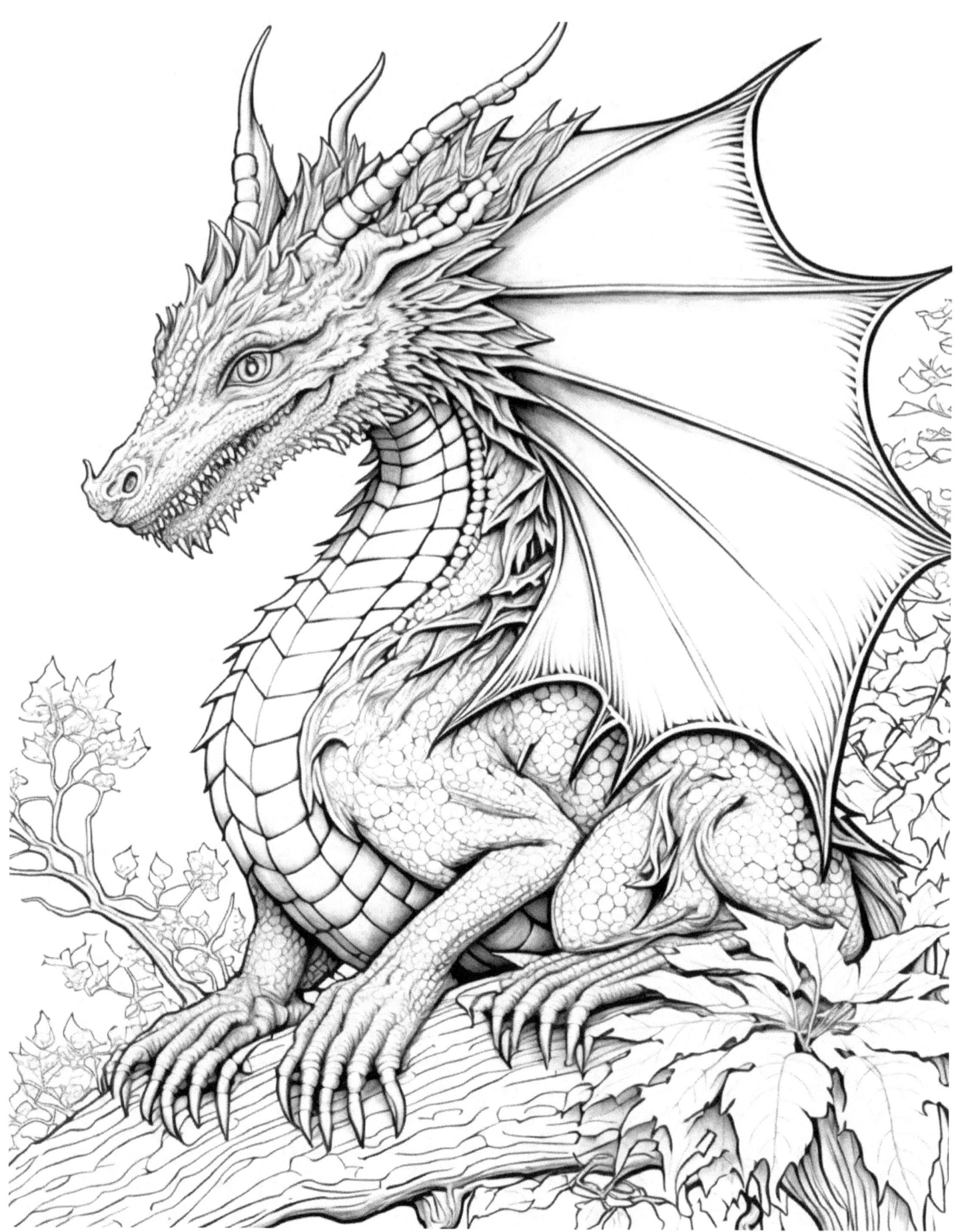

SPYING DRAGONS

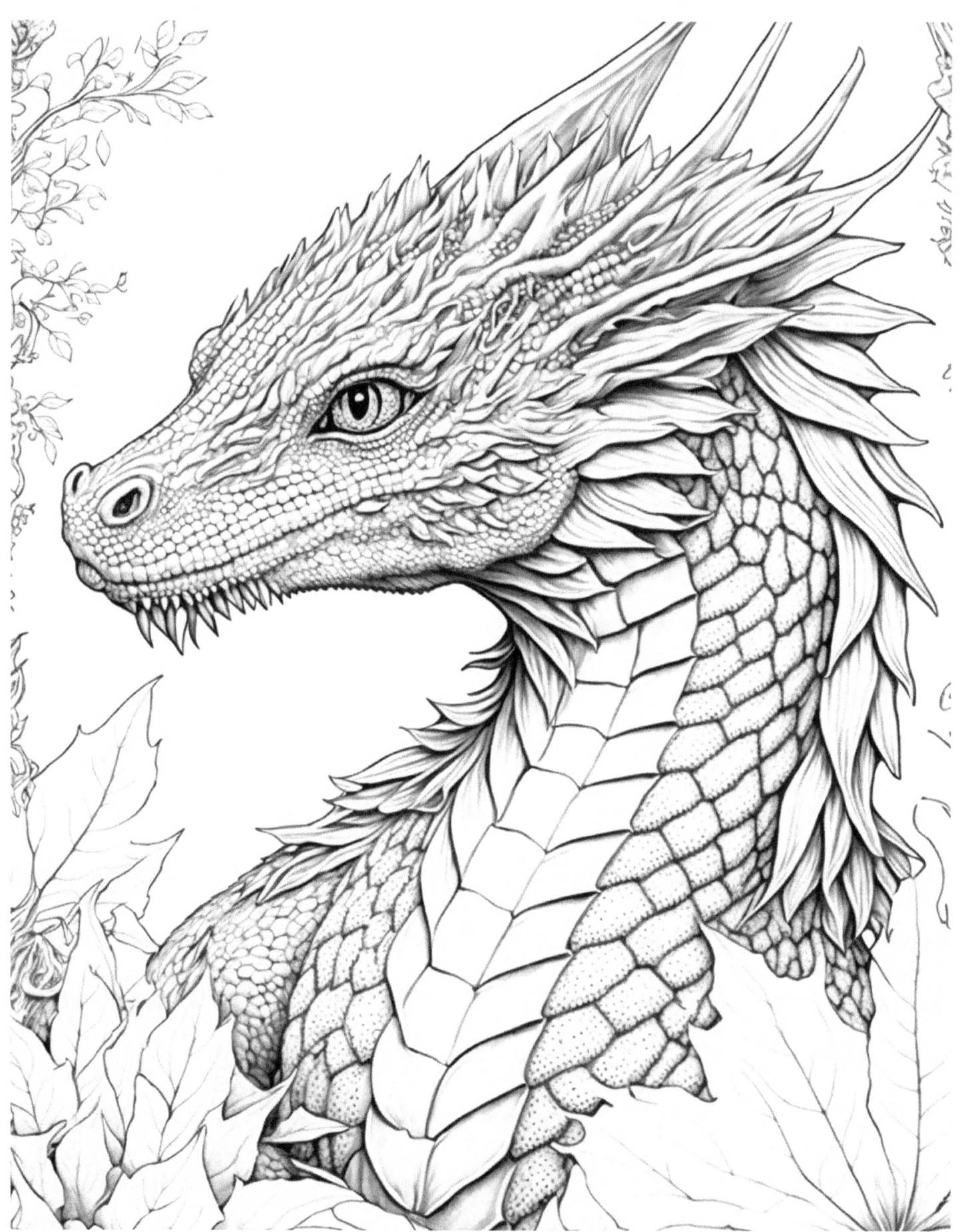

SPYING DRAGONS

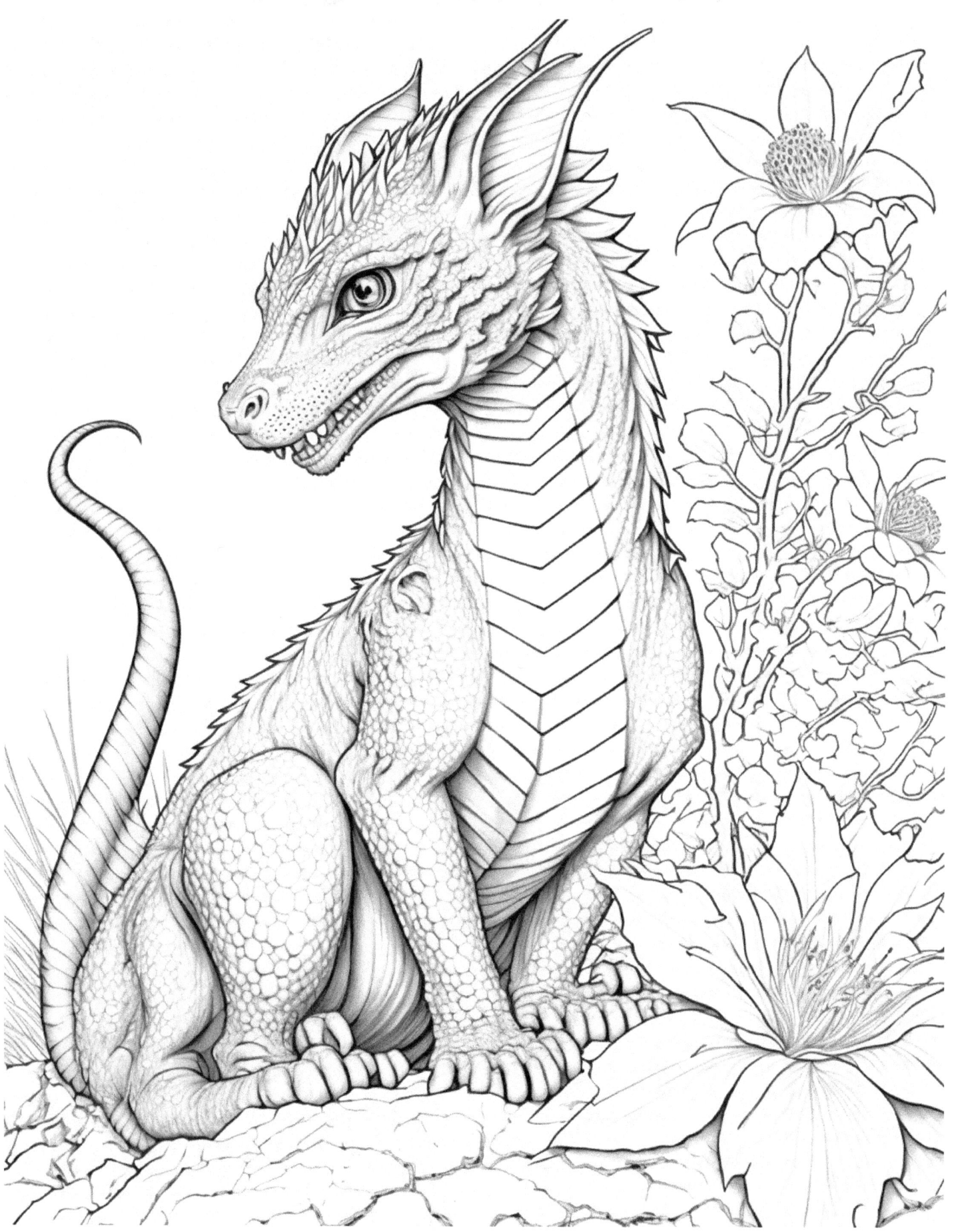

SPYING DRAGONS

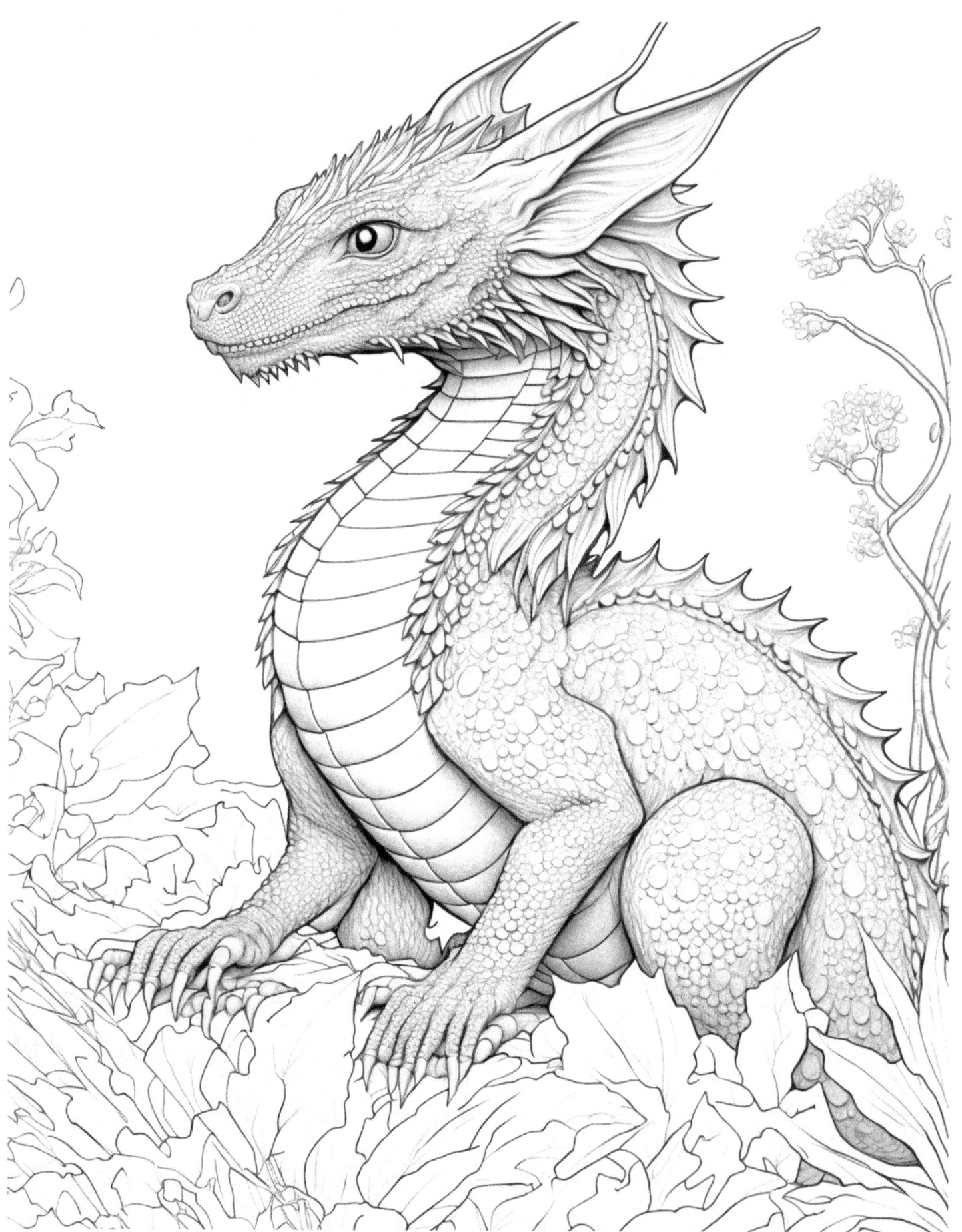

SPYING DRAGONS

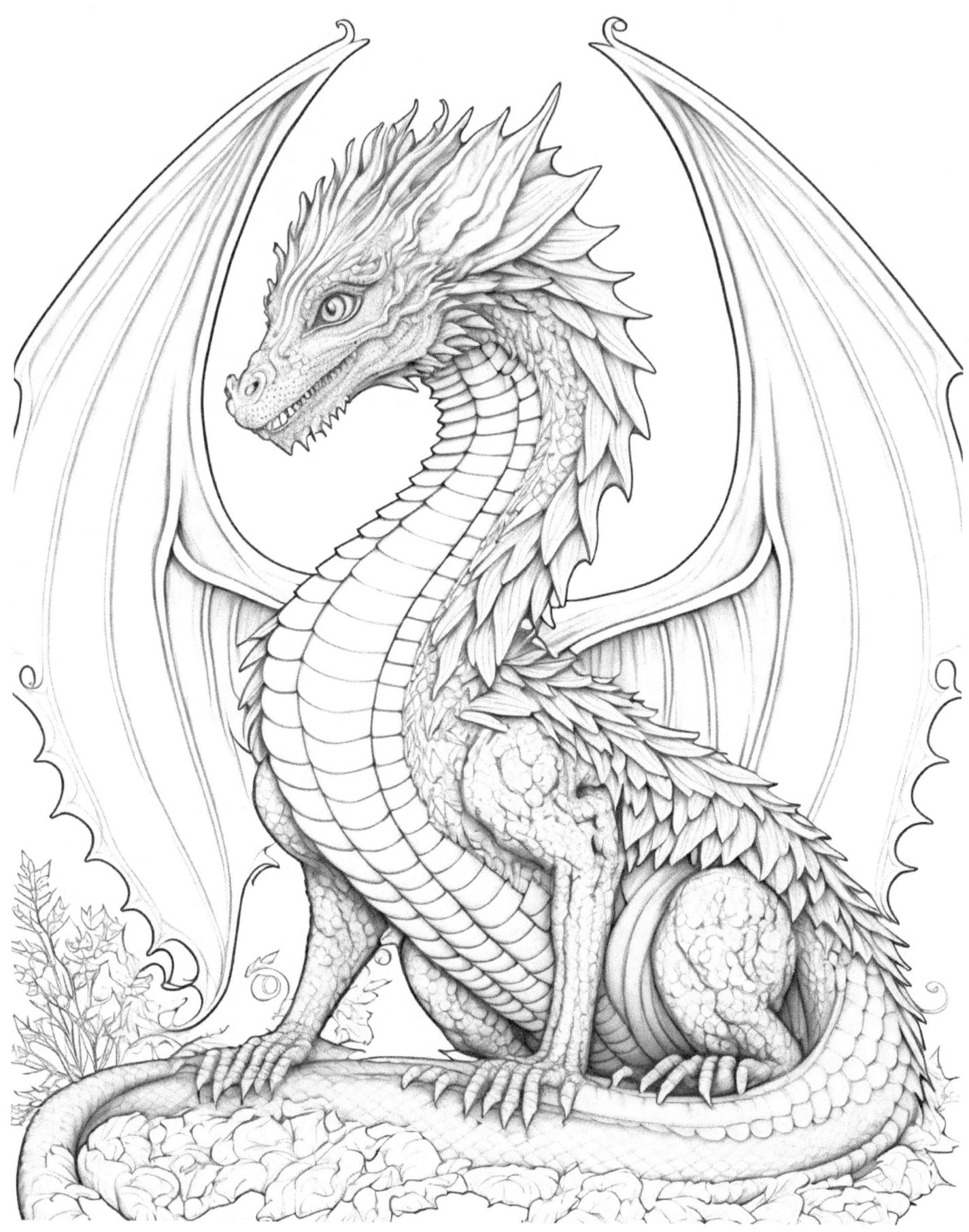

SPYING DRAGONS

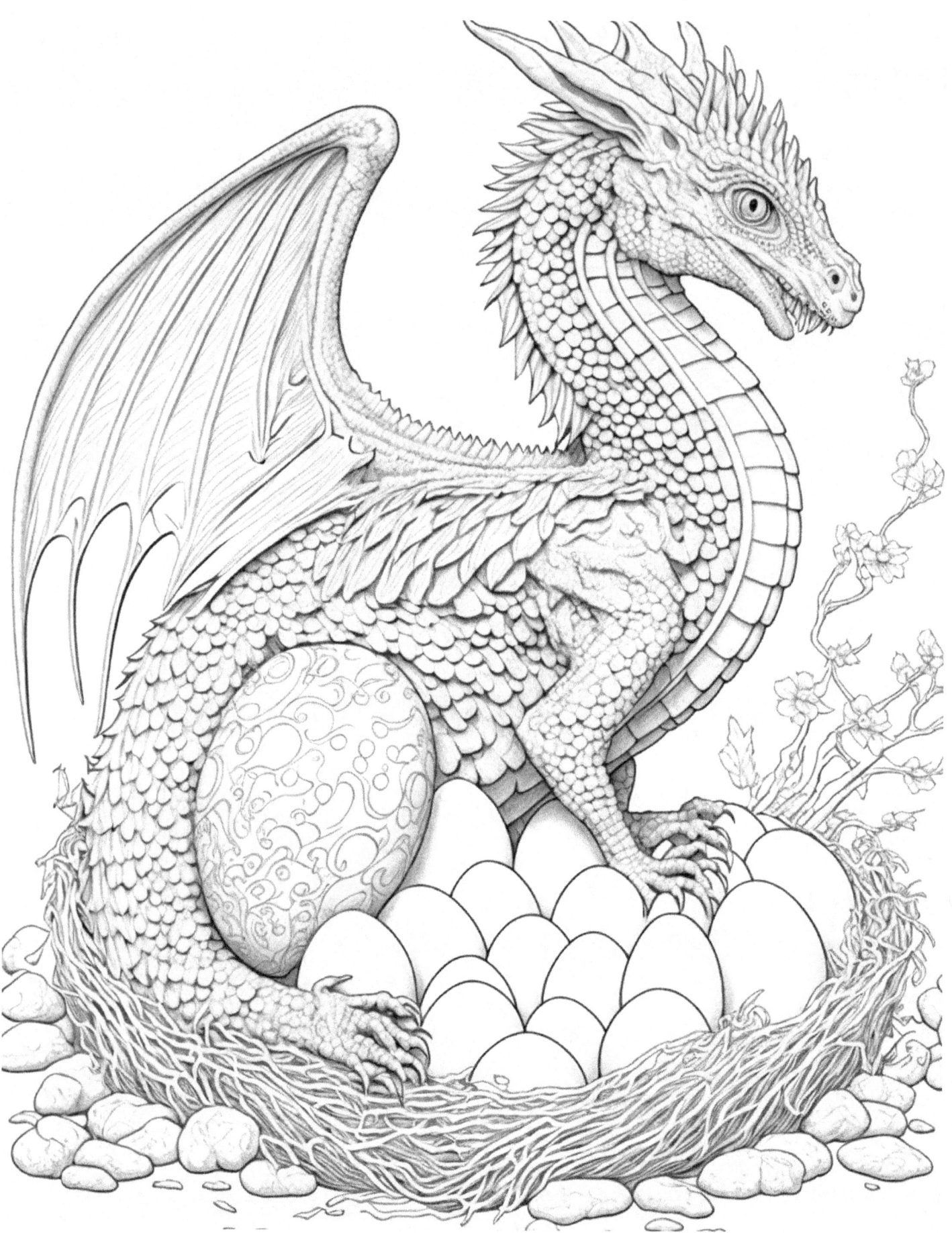

SPYING DRAGONS

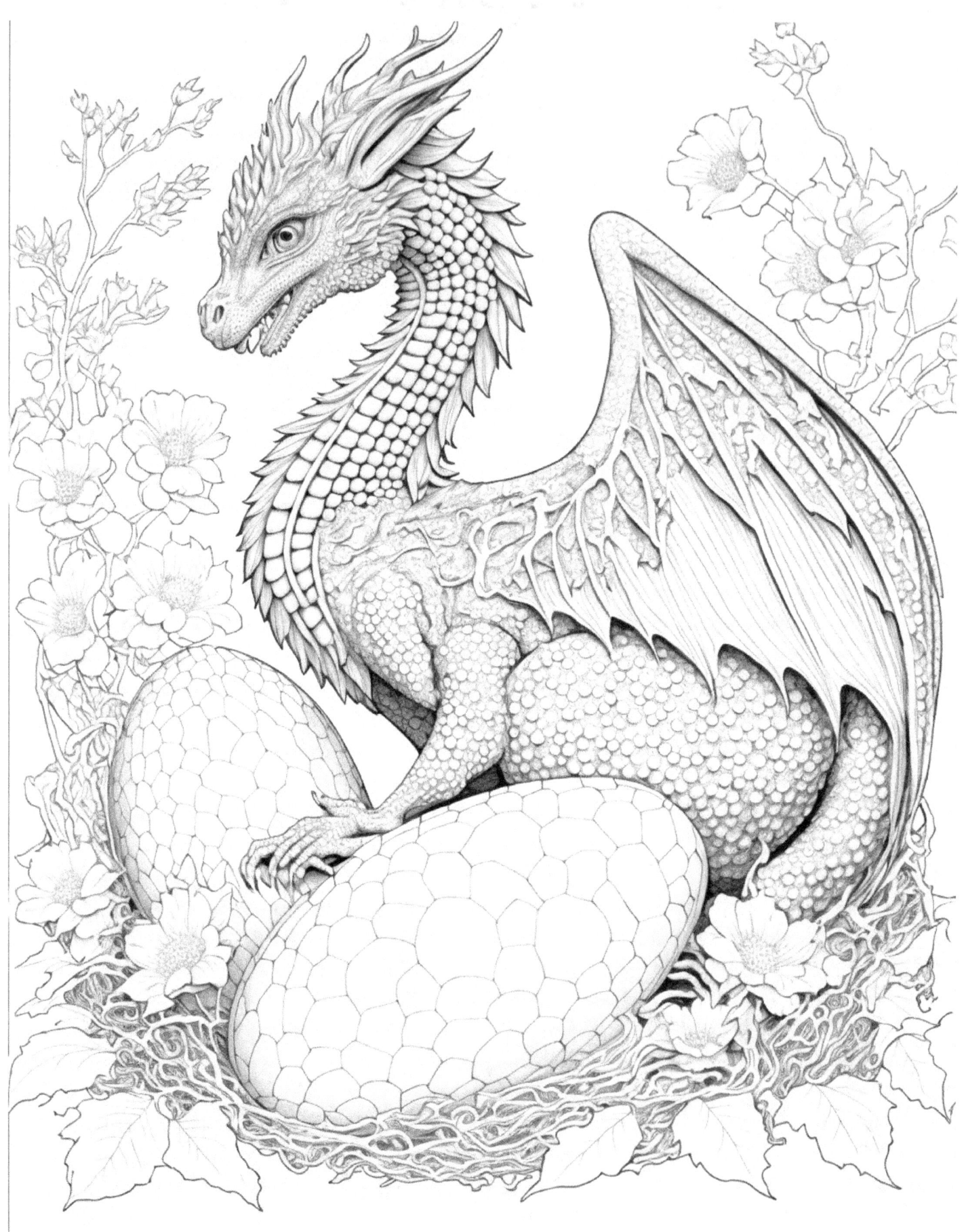

SPYING DRAGONS

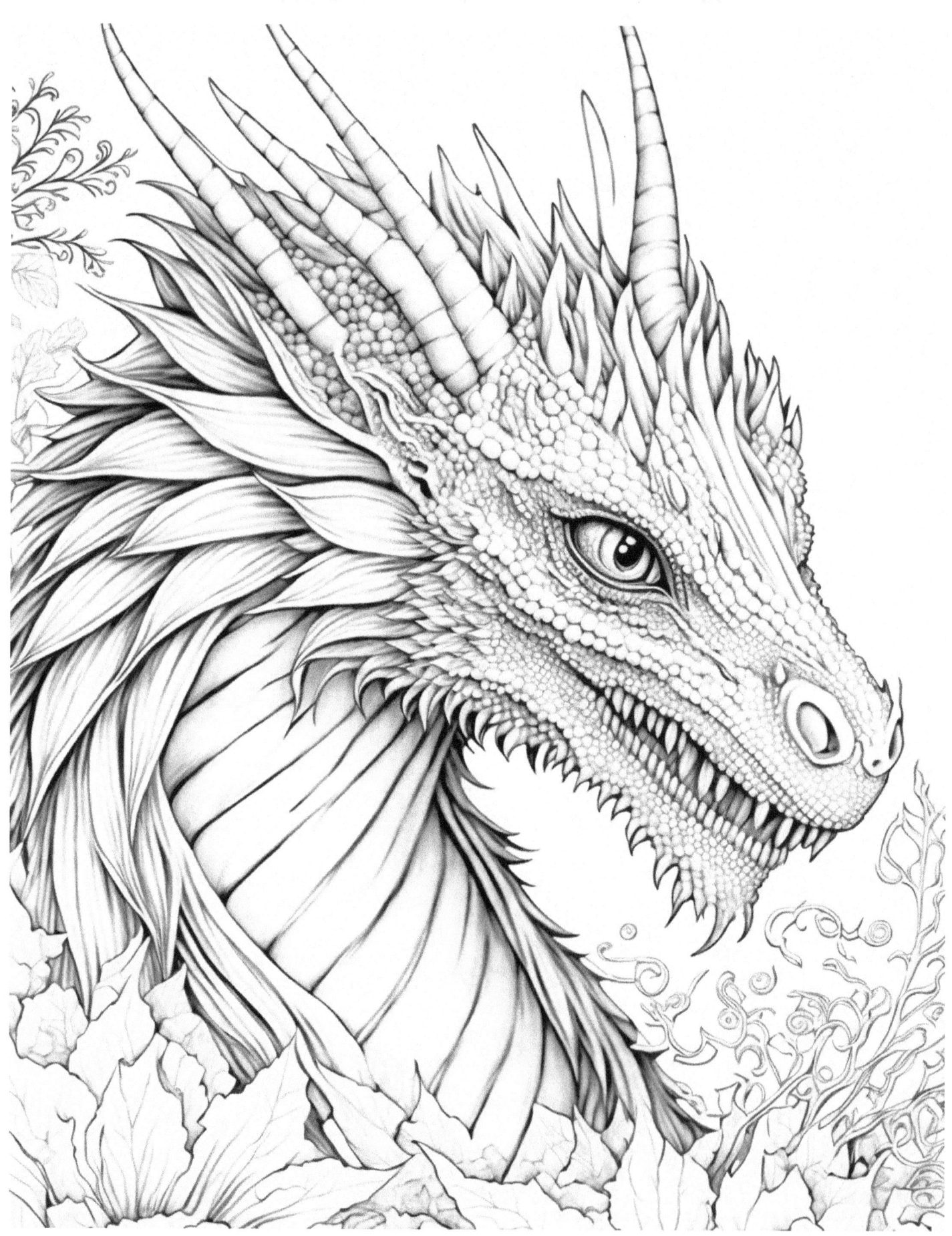

SPYING DRAGONS

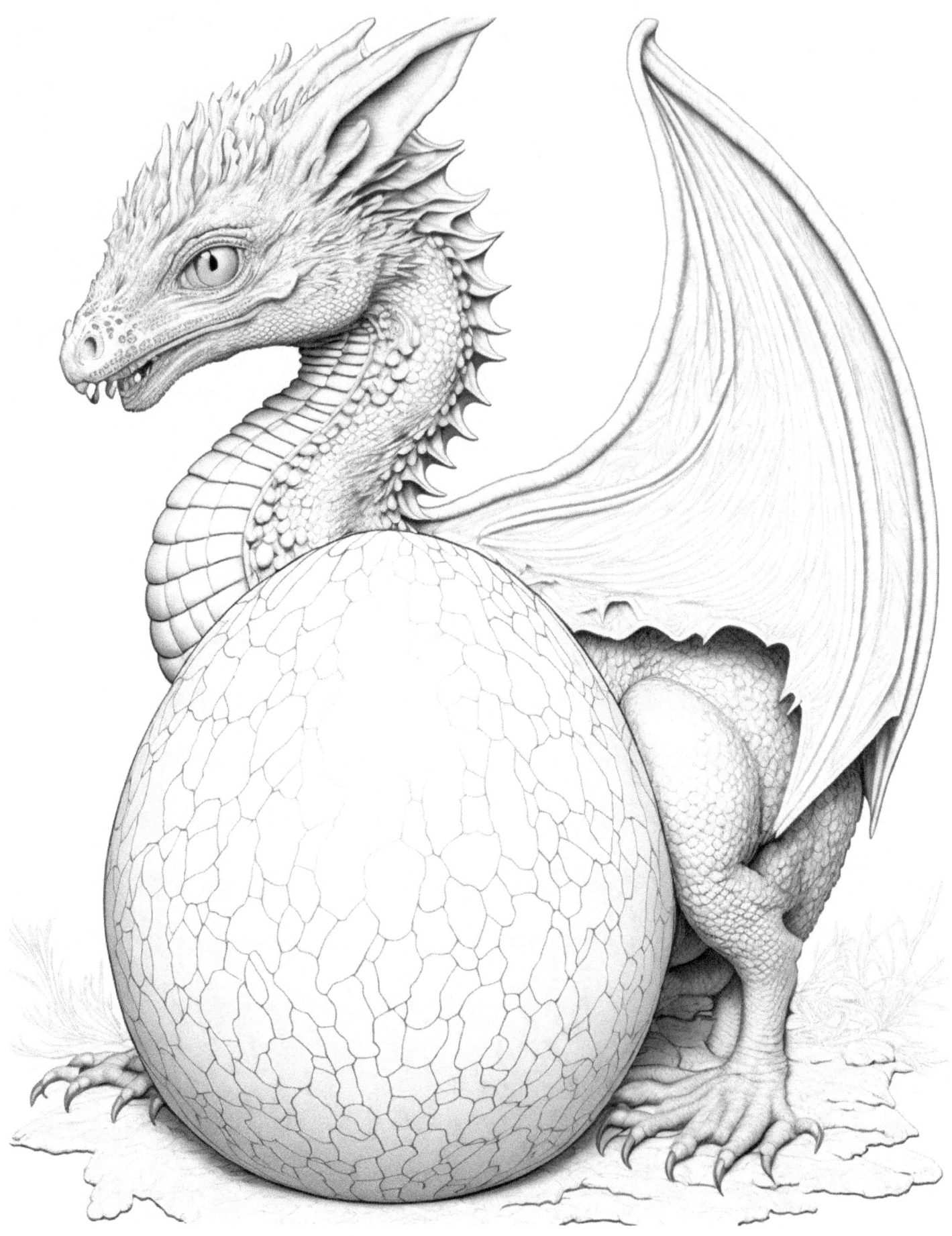

SPYING DRAGONS

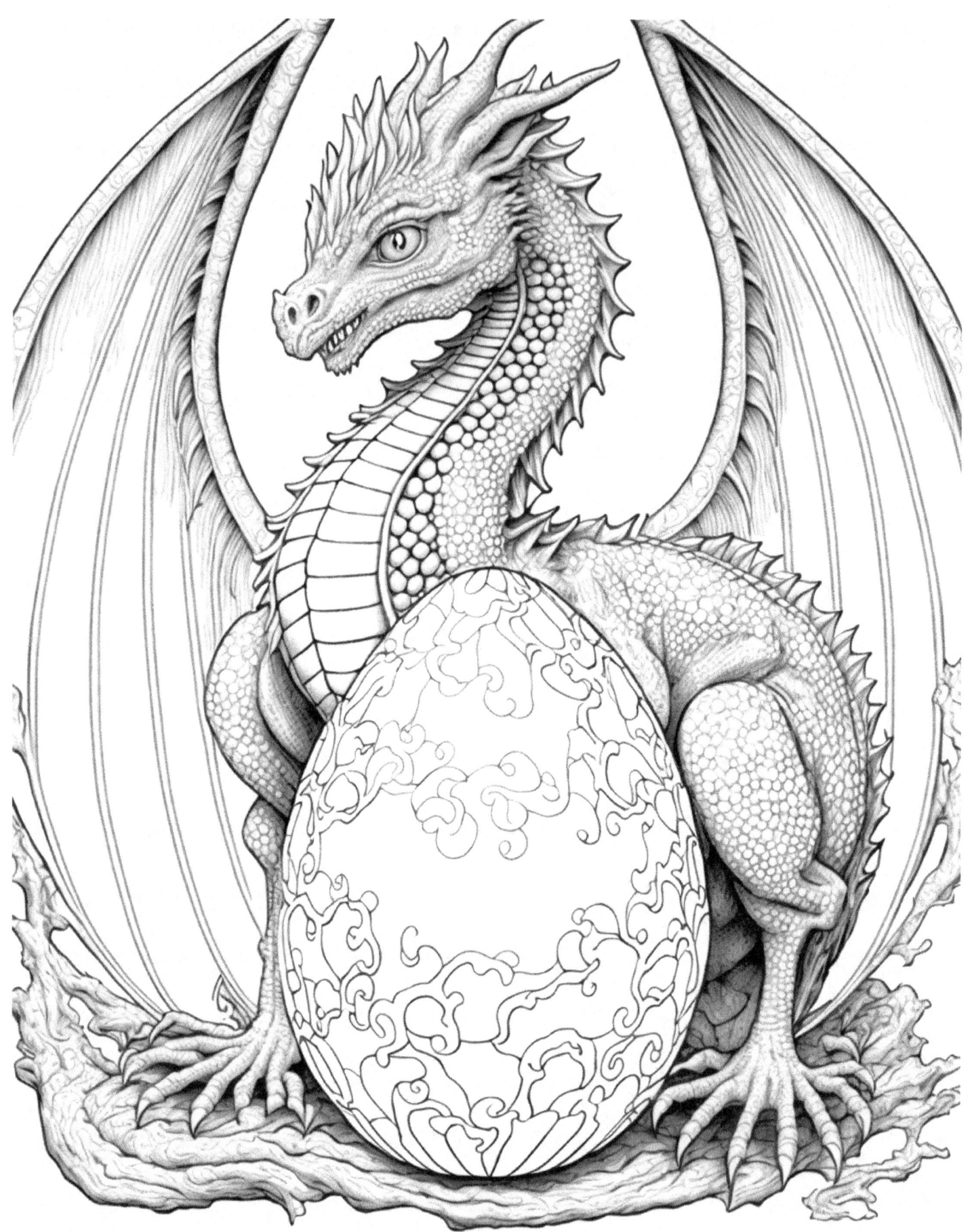

SPYING DRAGONS

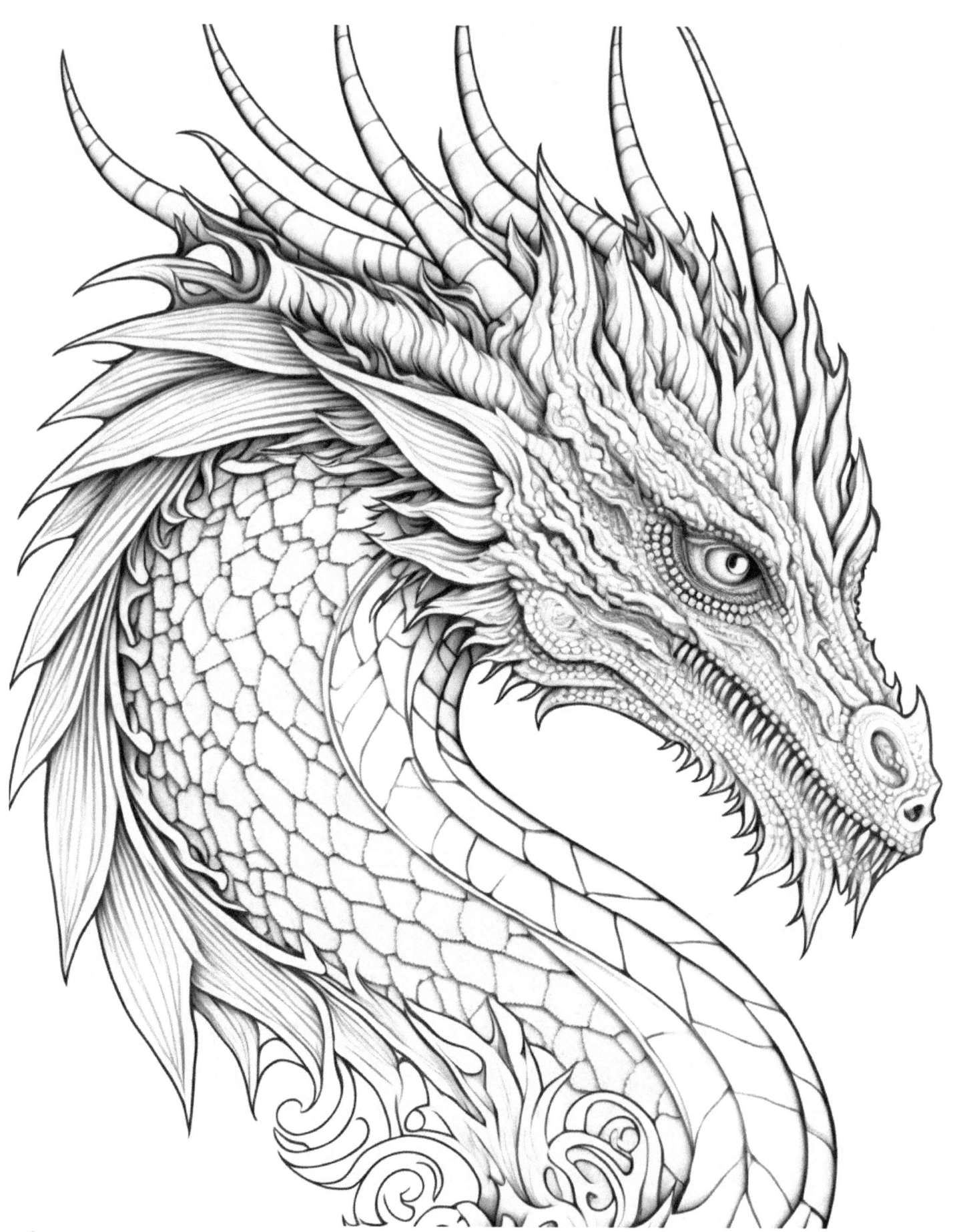

SPYING DRAGONS

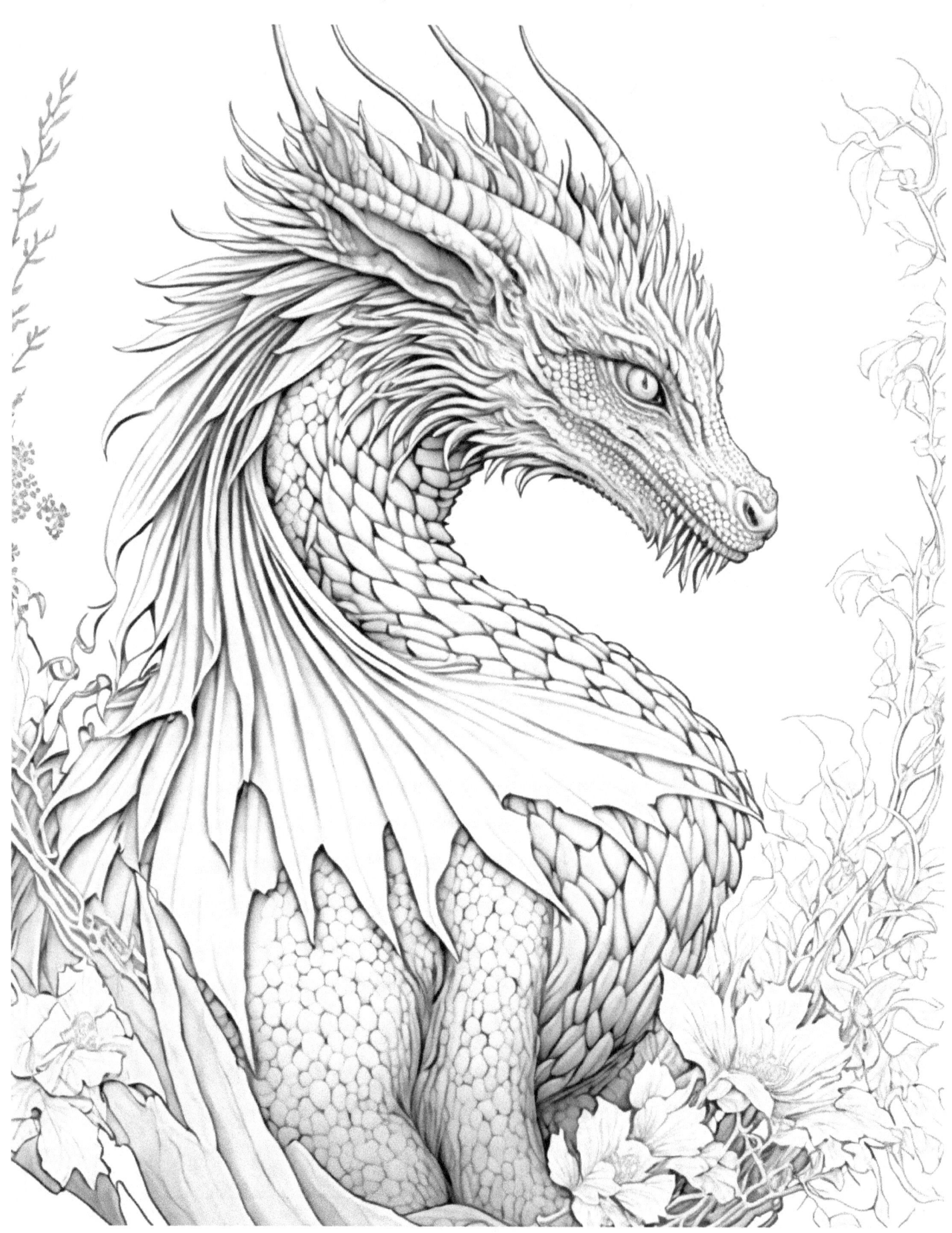

SPYING DRAGONS

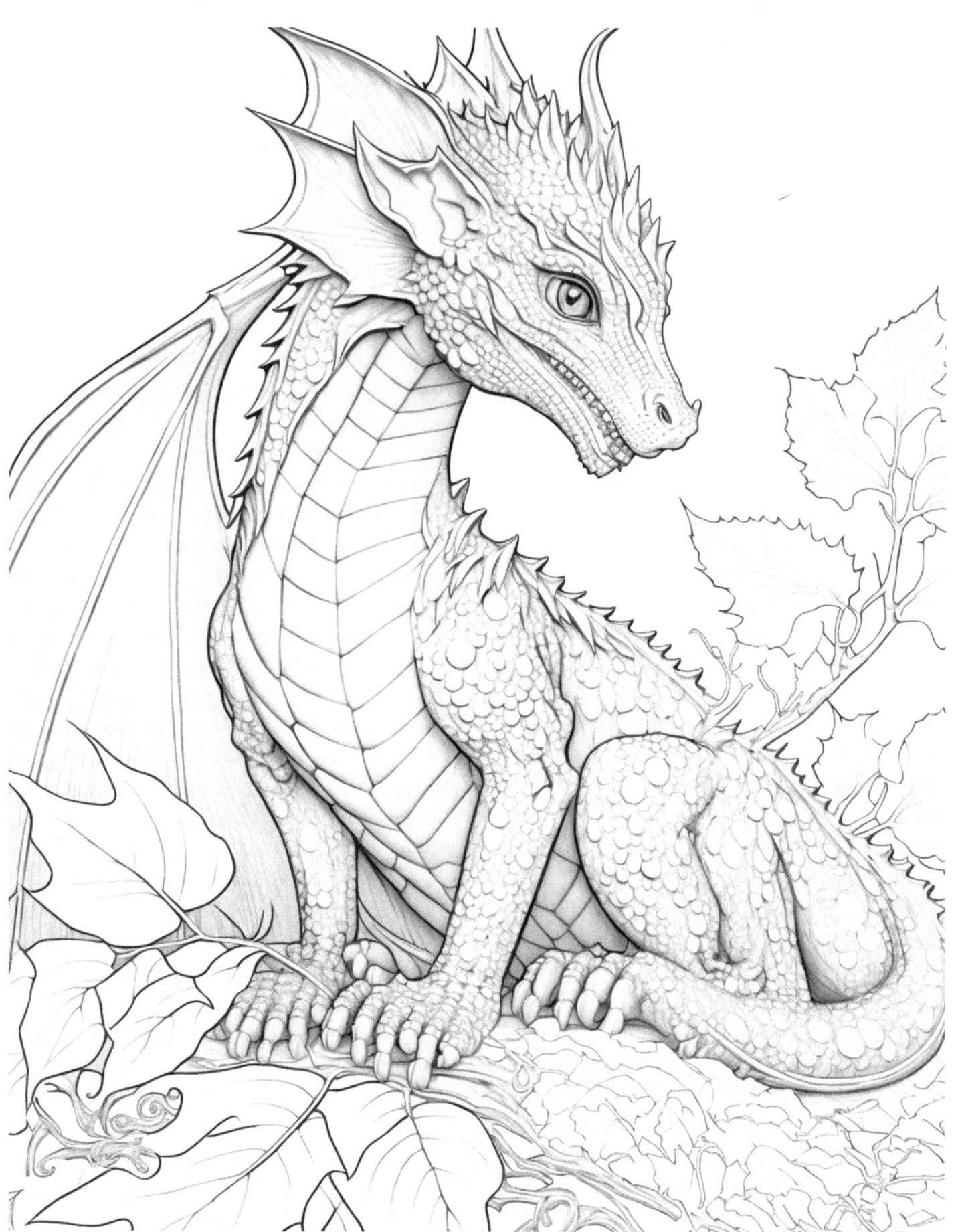

SPYING DRAGONS

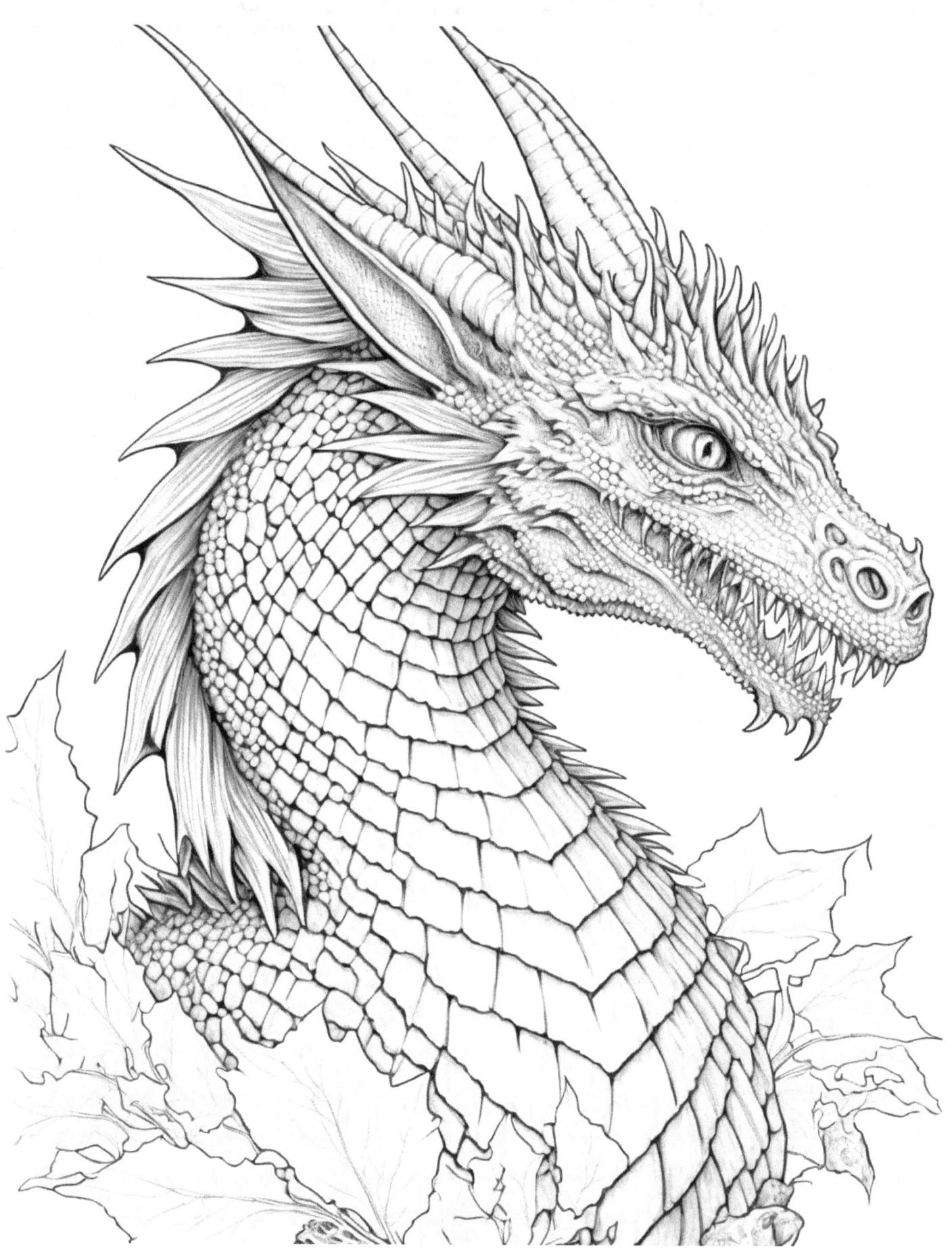

SPYING DRAGONS

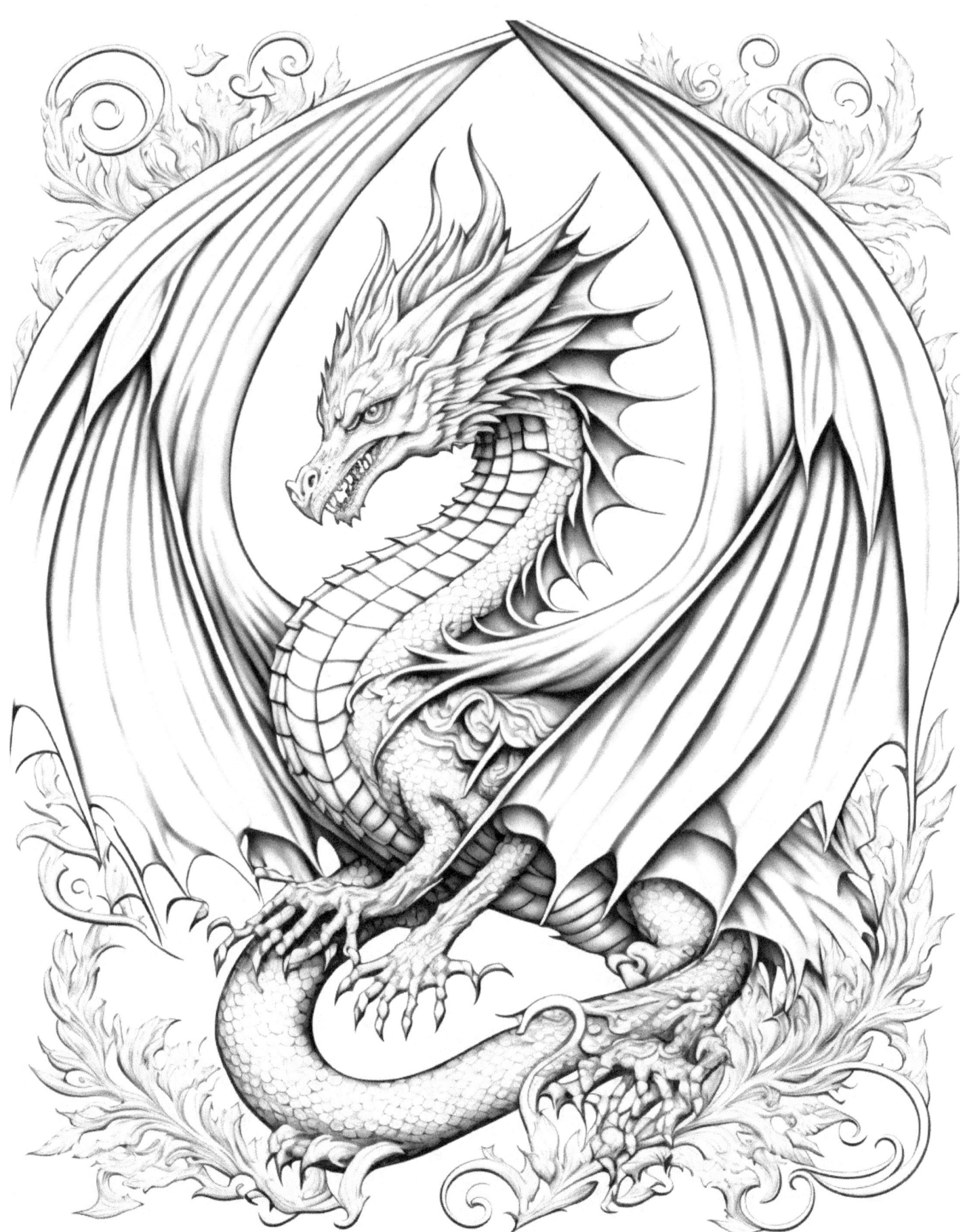

SPYING DRAGONS

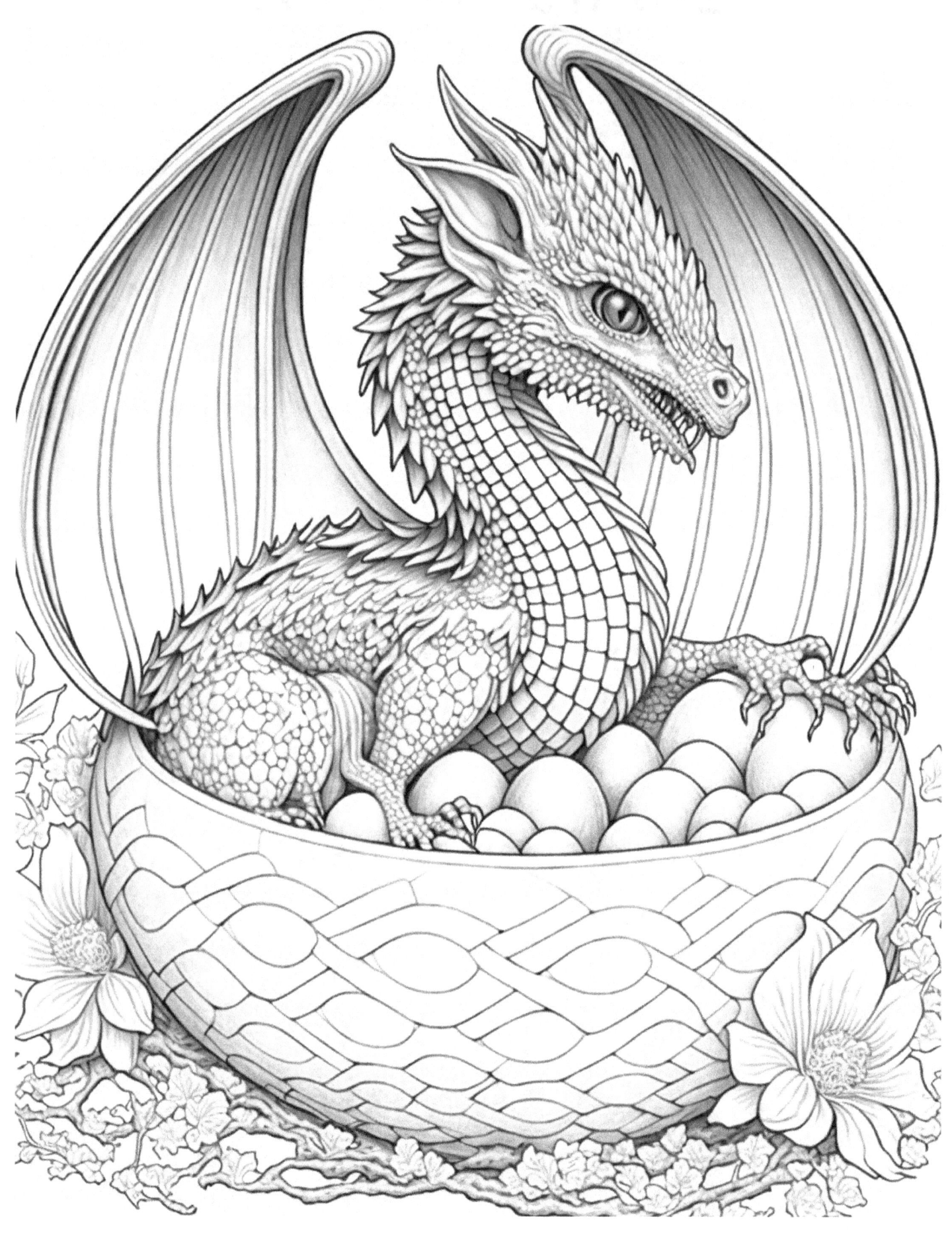

SPYING DRAGONS

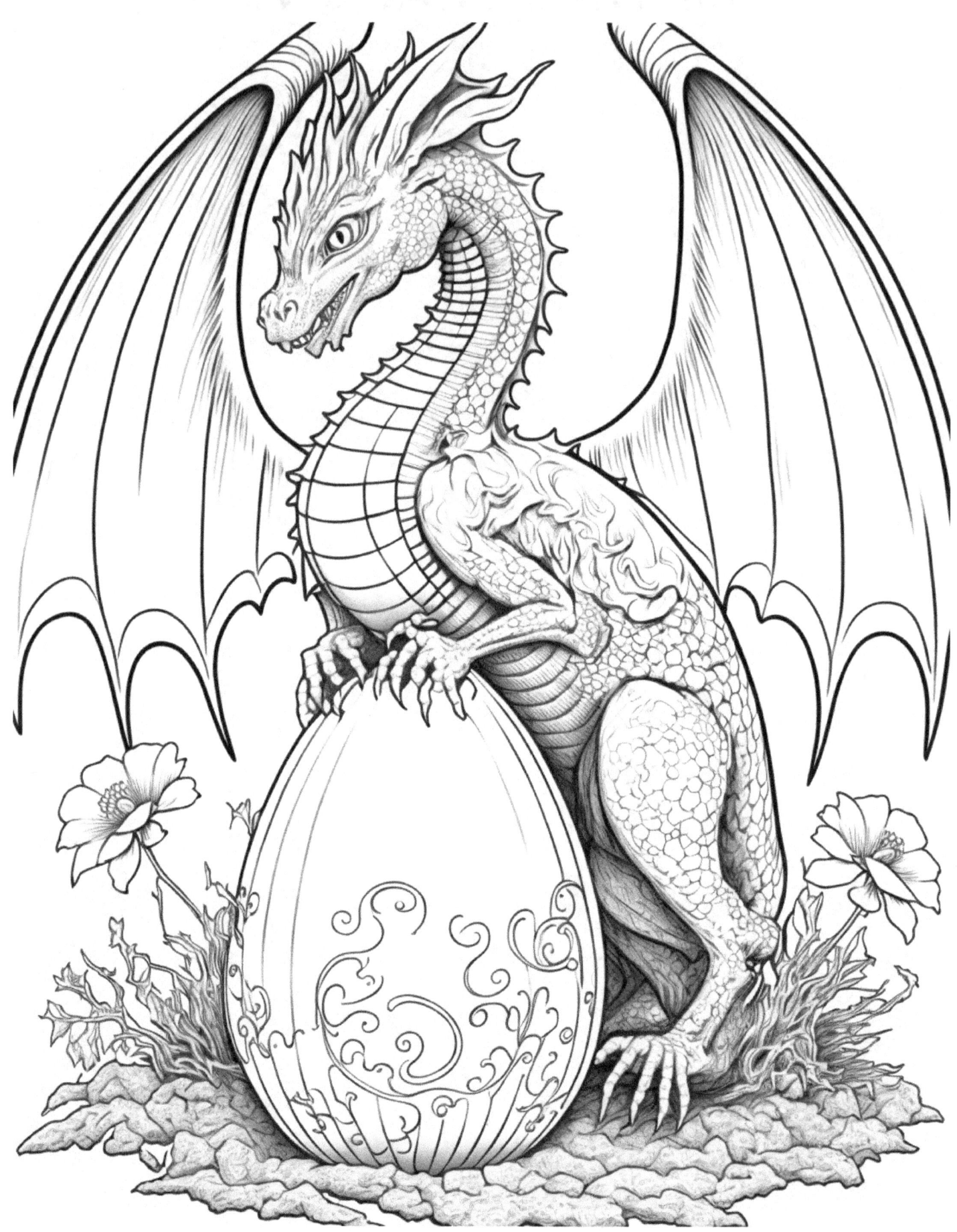

SPYING DRAGONS

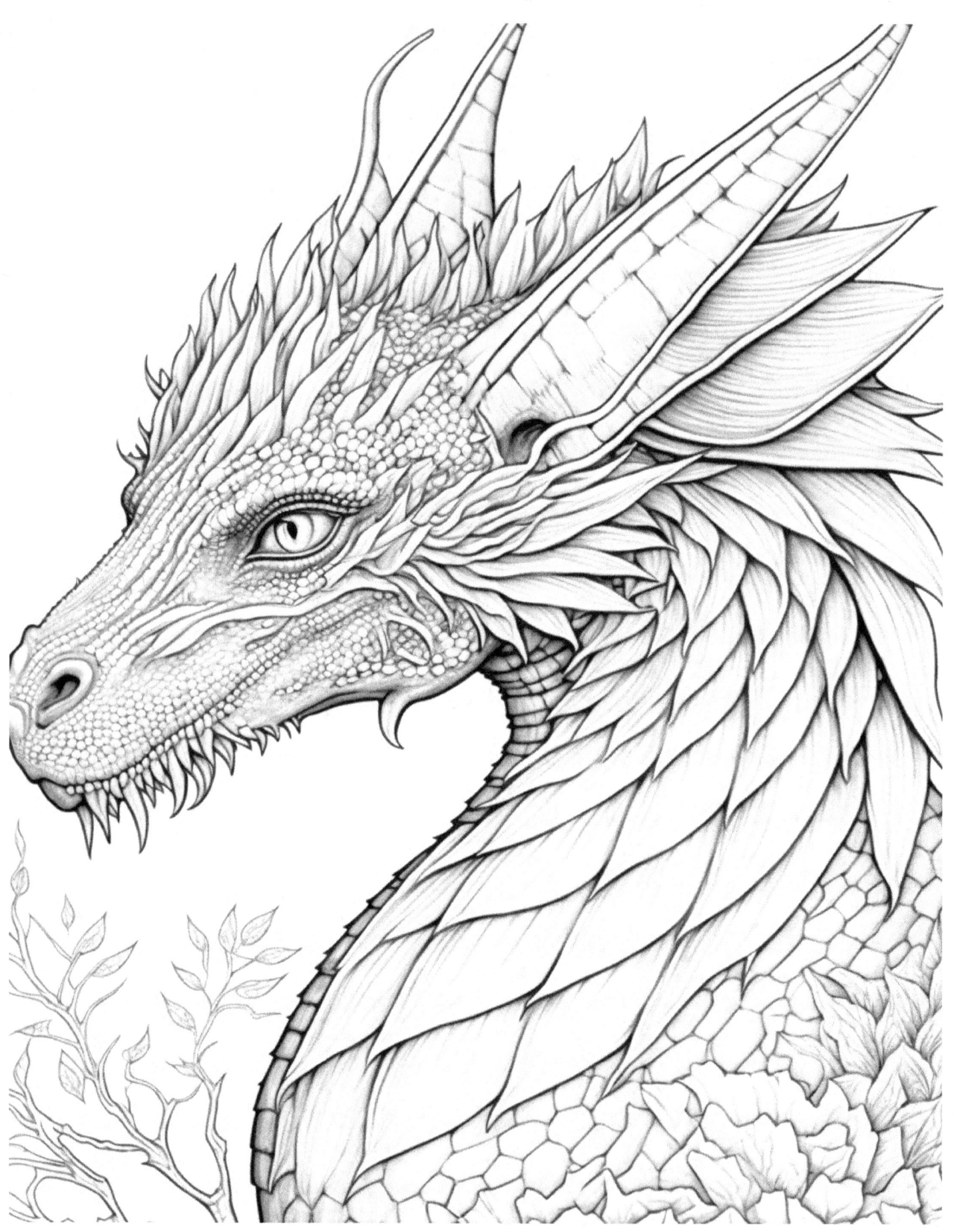

SPYING DRAGONS

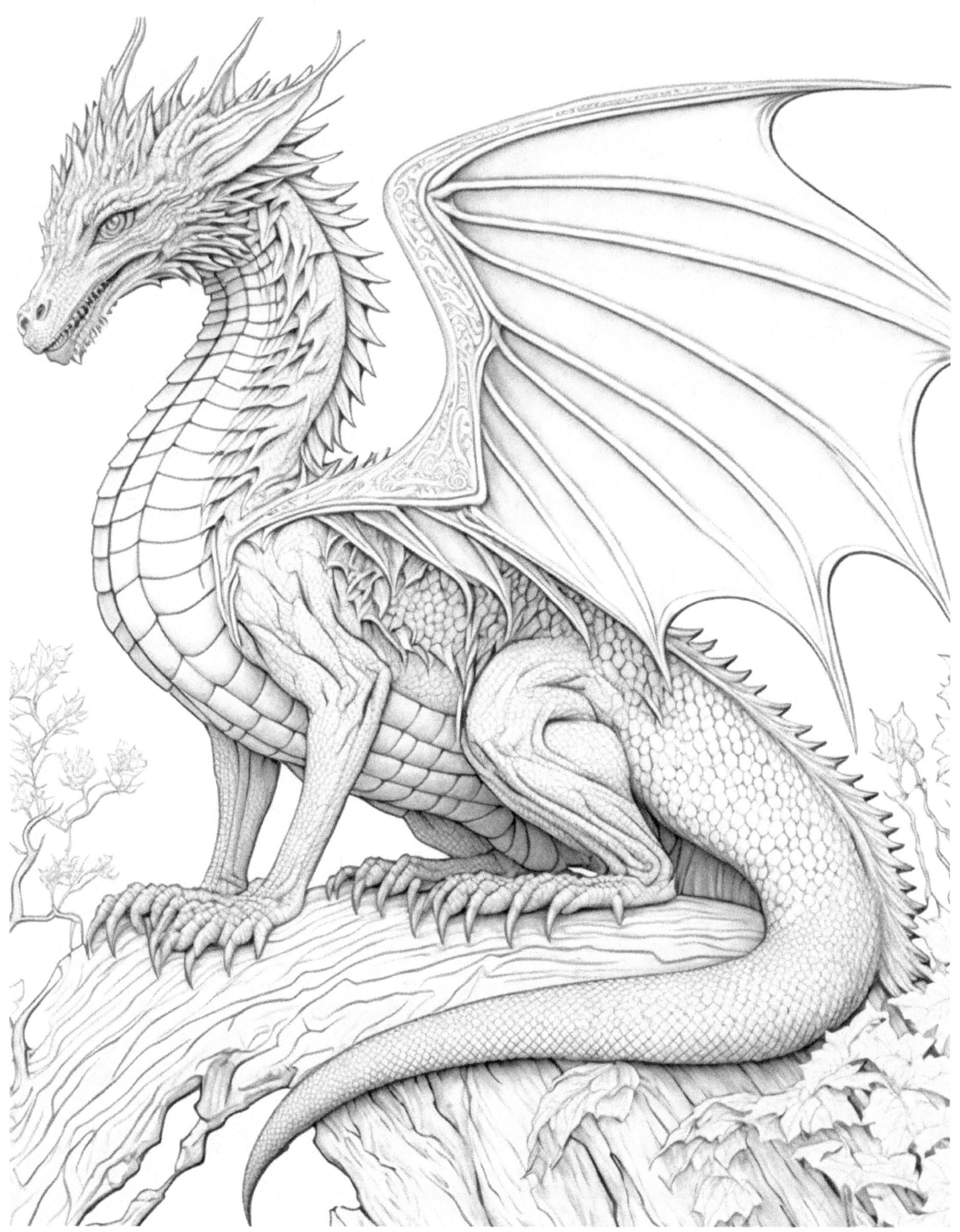

SPYING DRAGONS

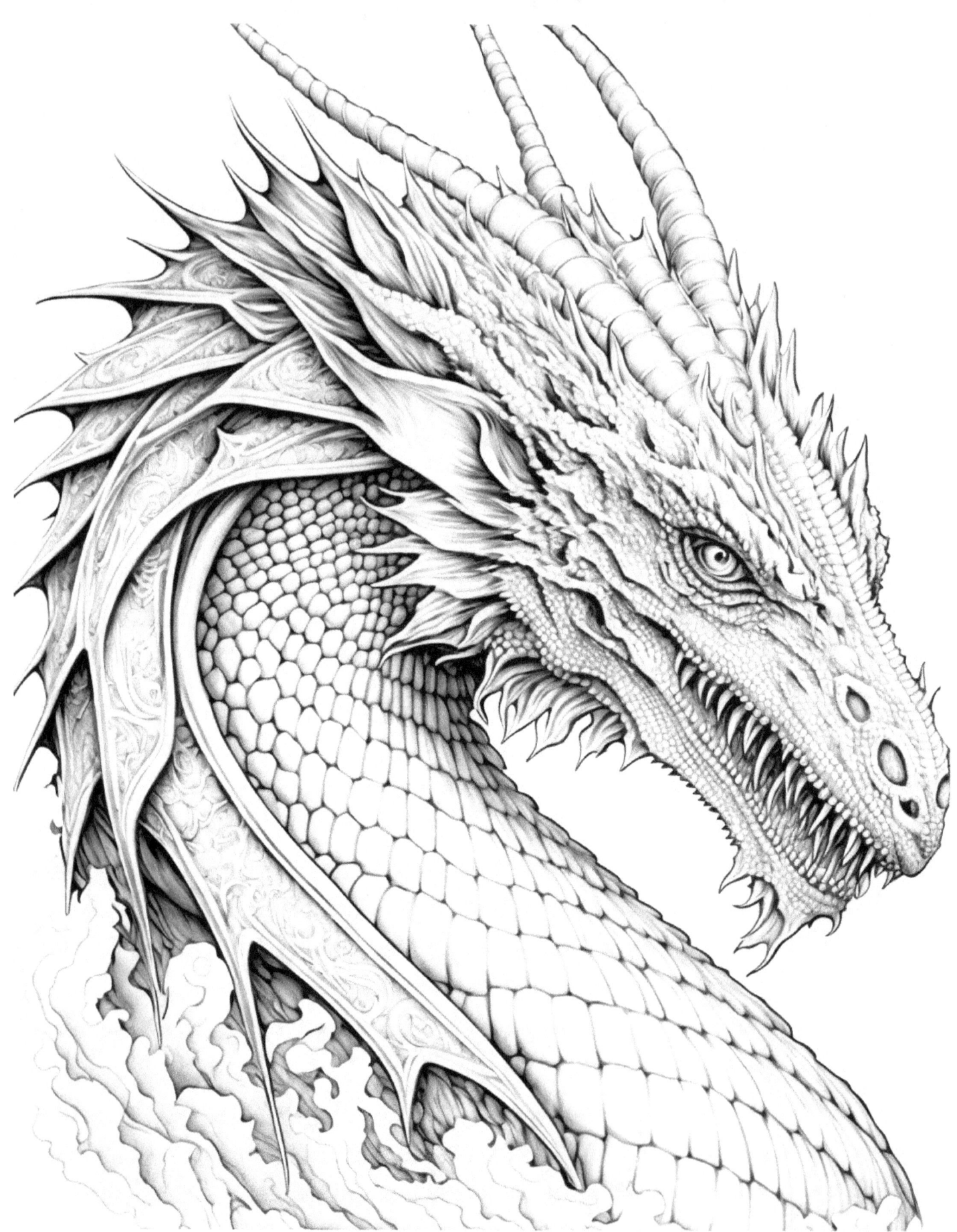

SPYING DRAGONS

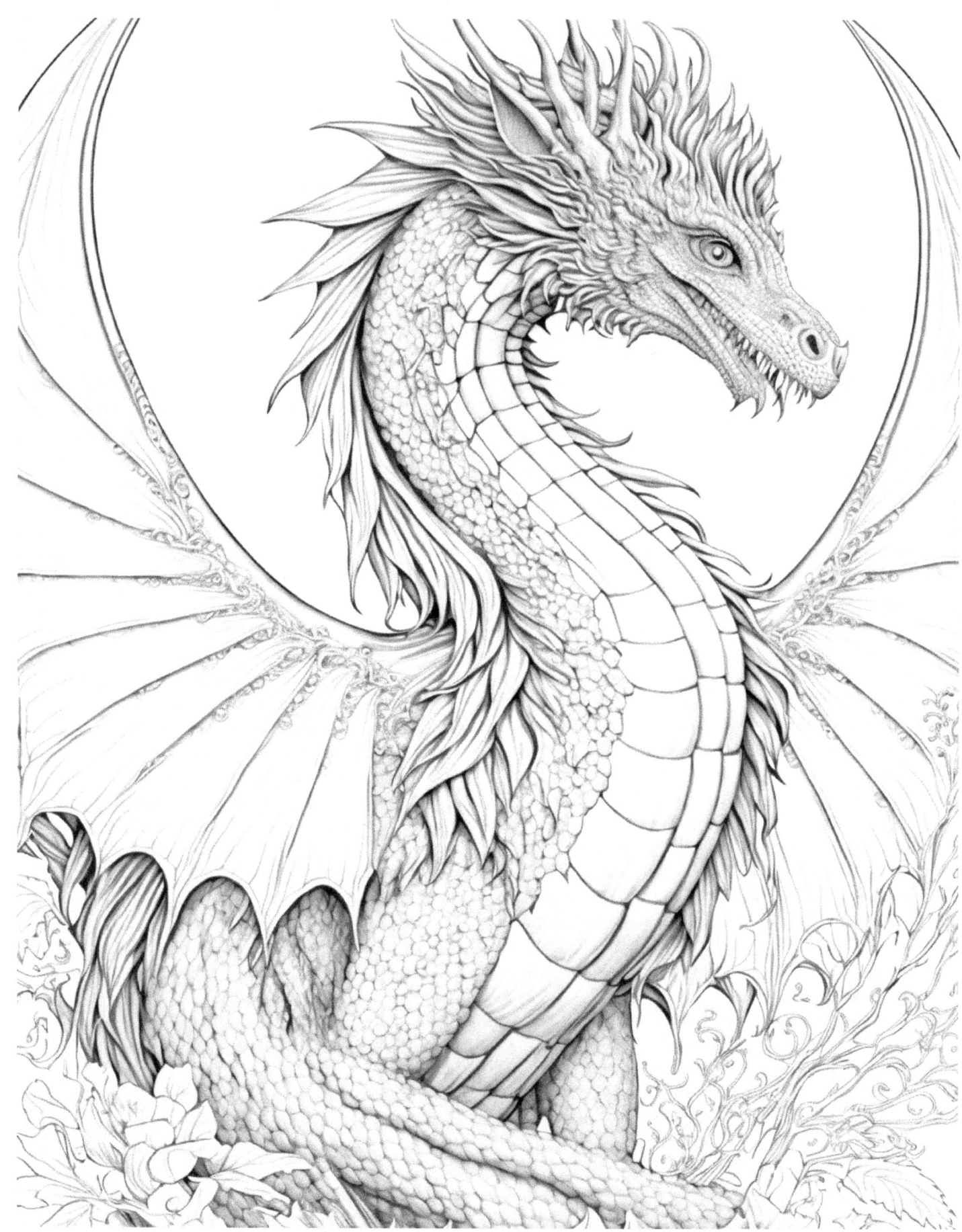

SPYING DRAGONS

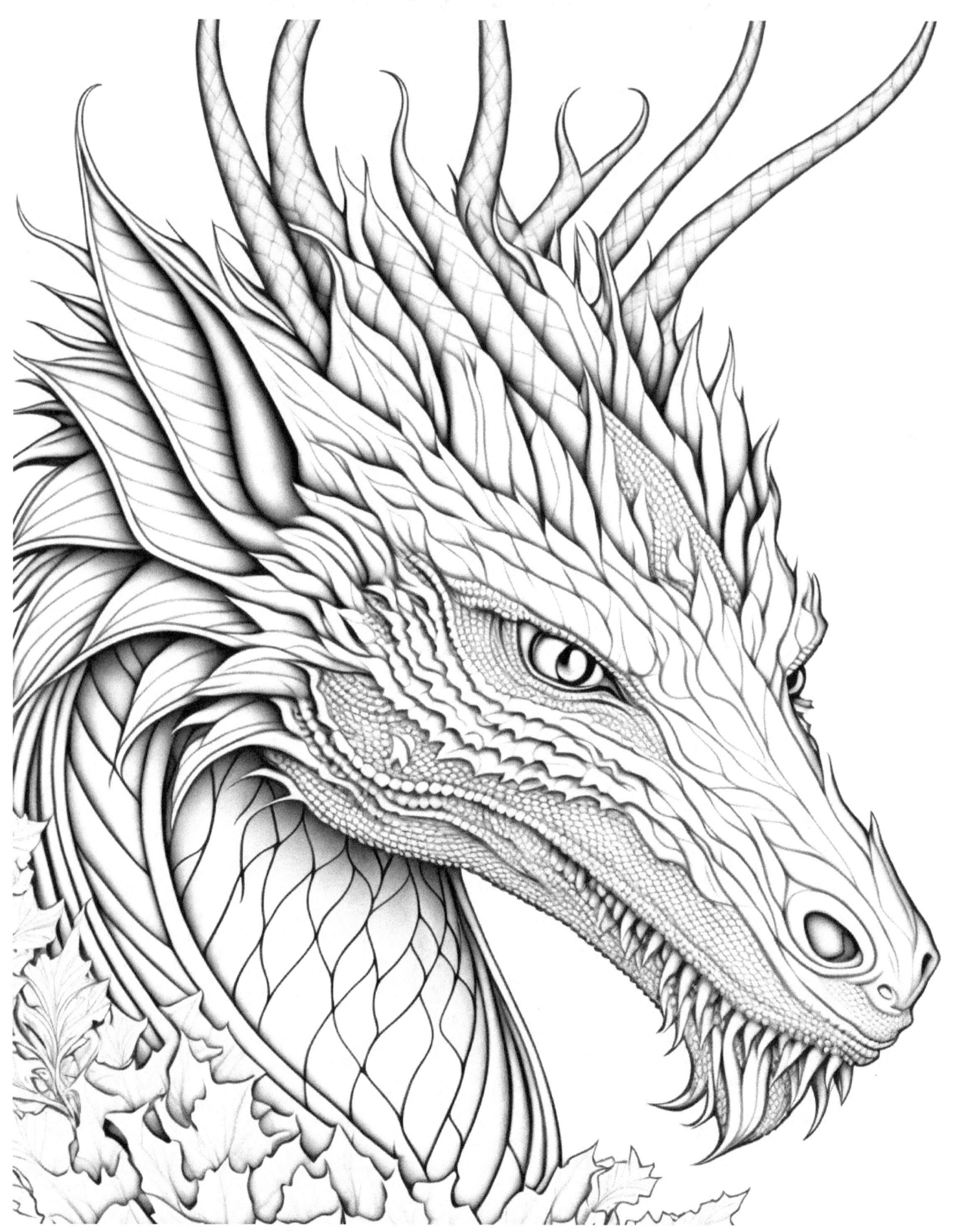

SPYING DRAGONS

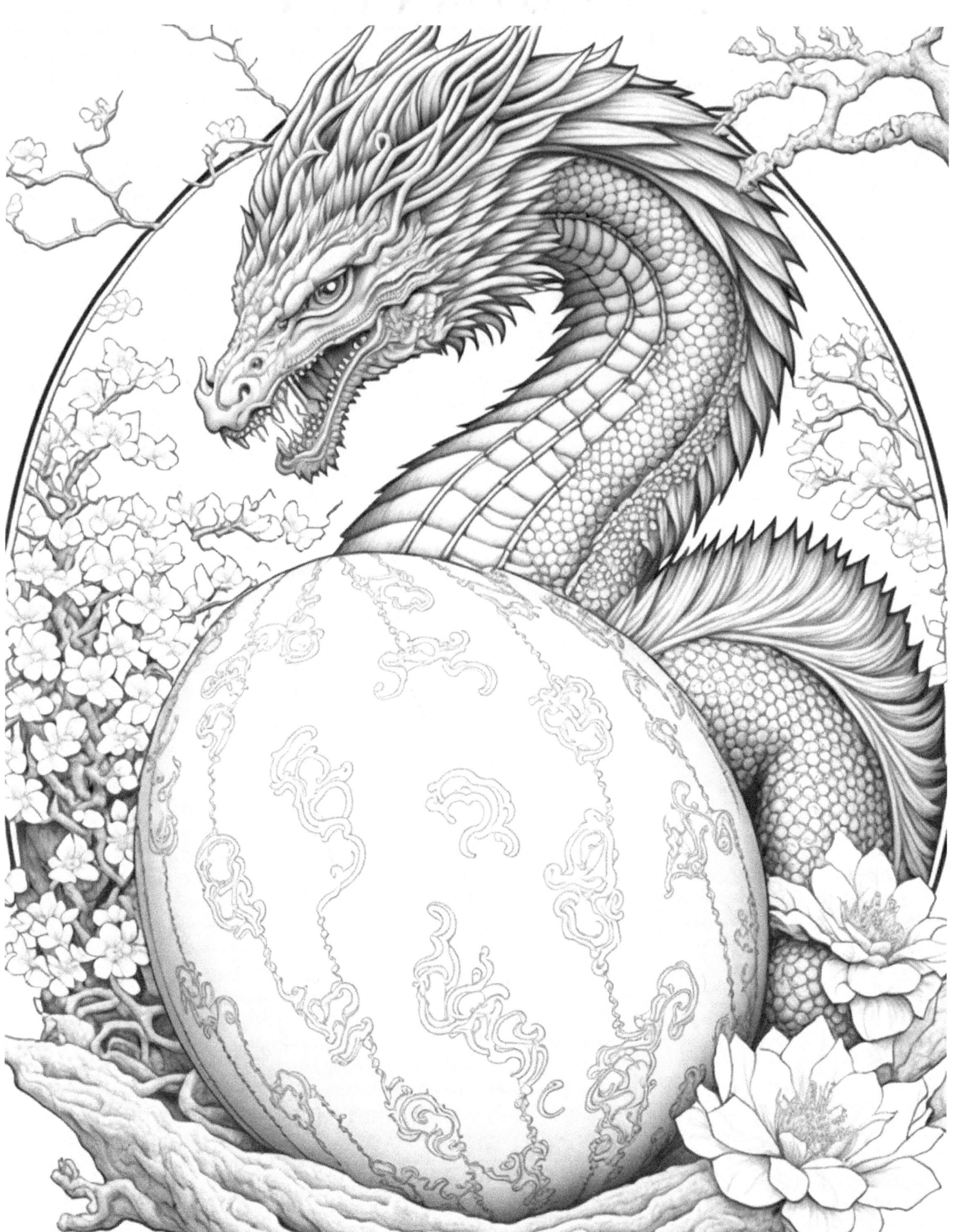

SPYING DRAGONS

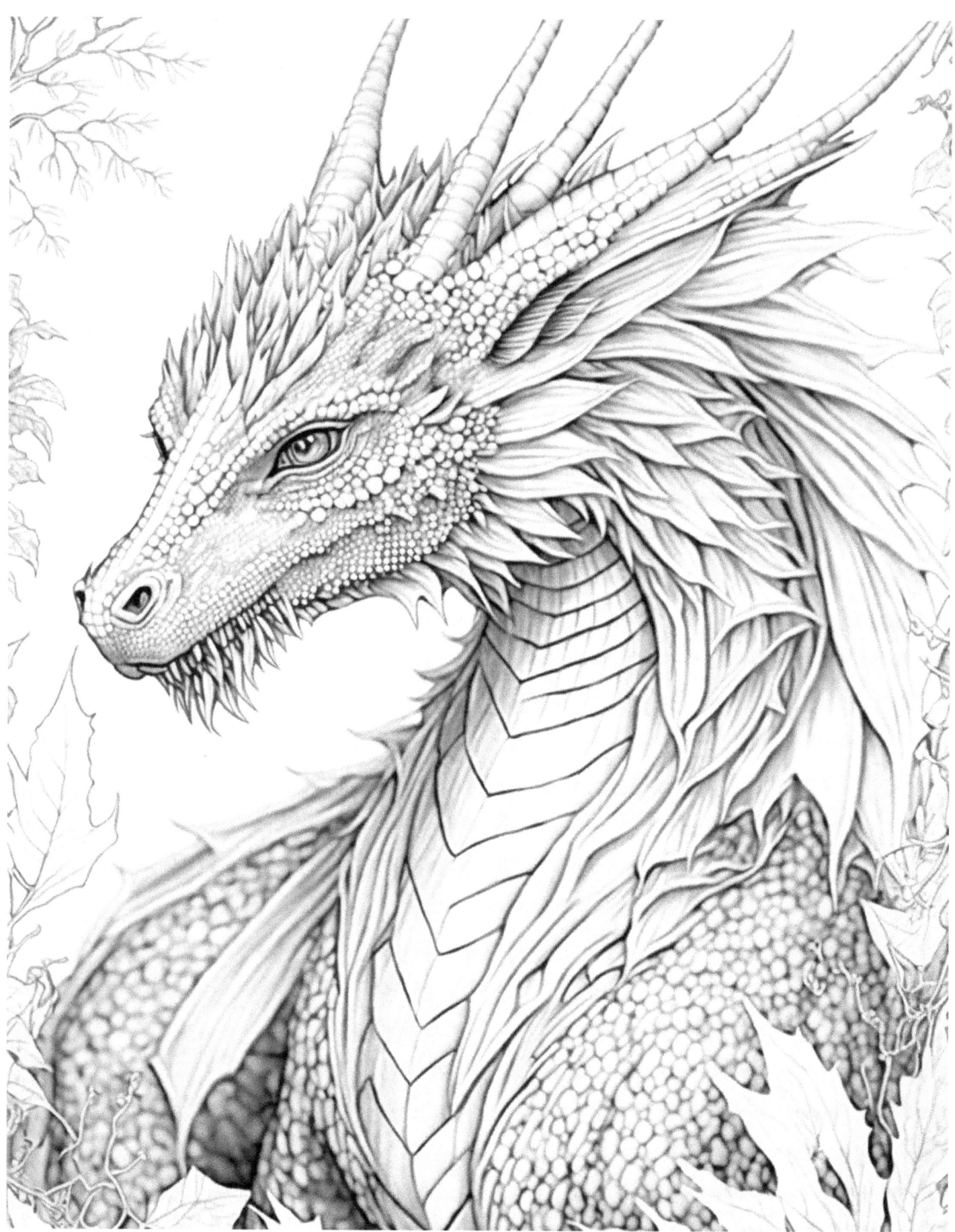

SPYING DRAGONS

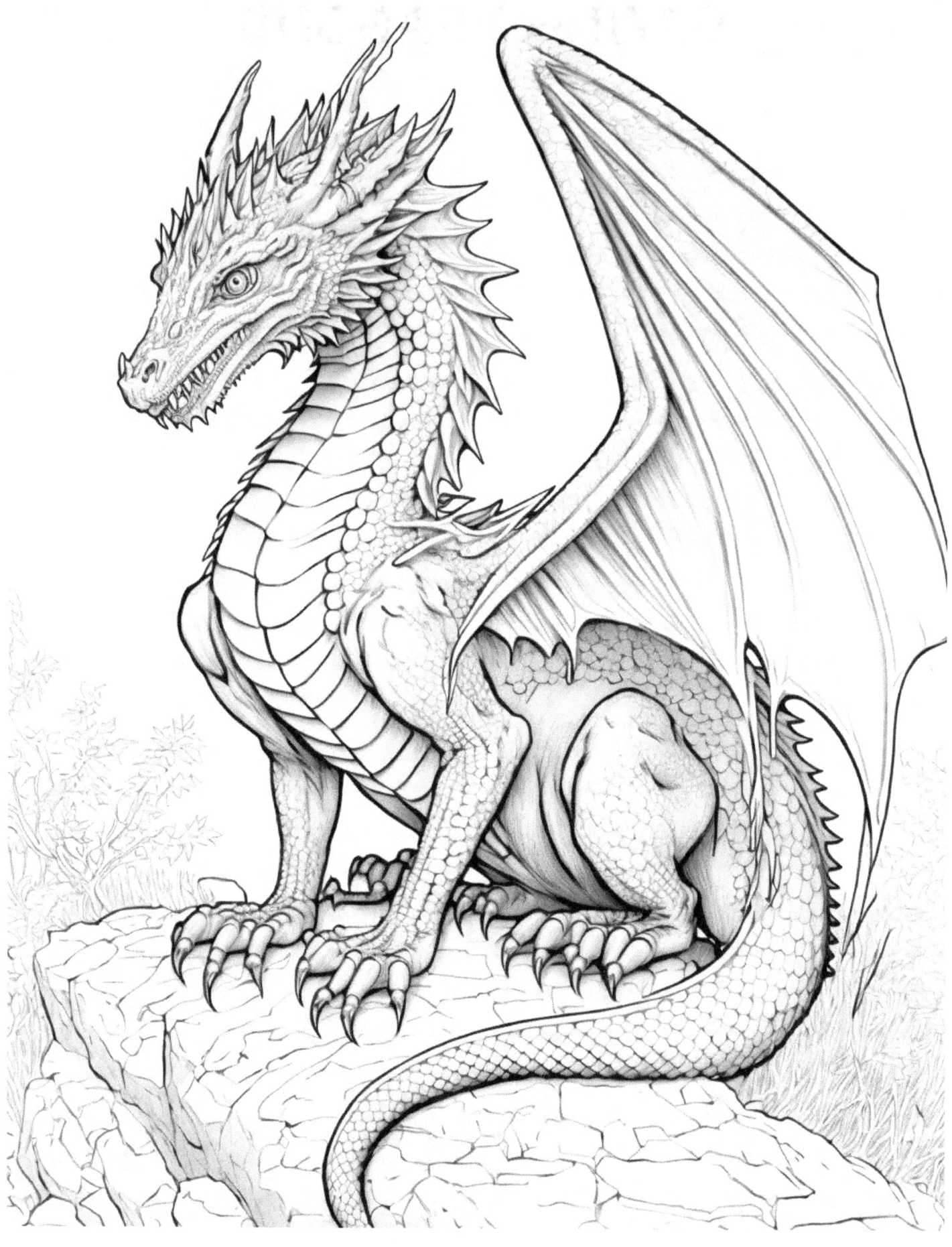

SPYING DRAGONS

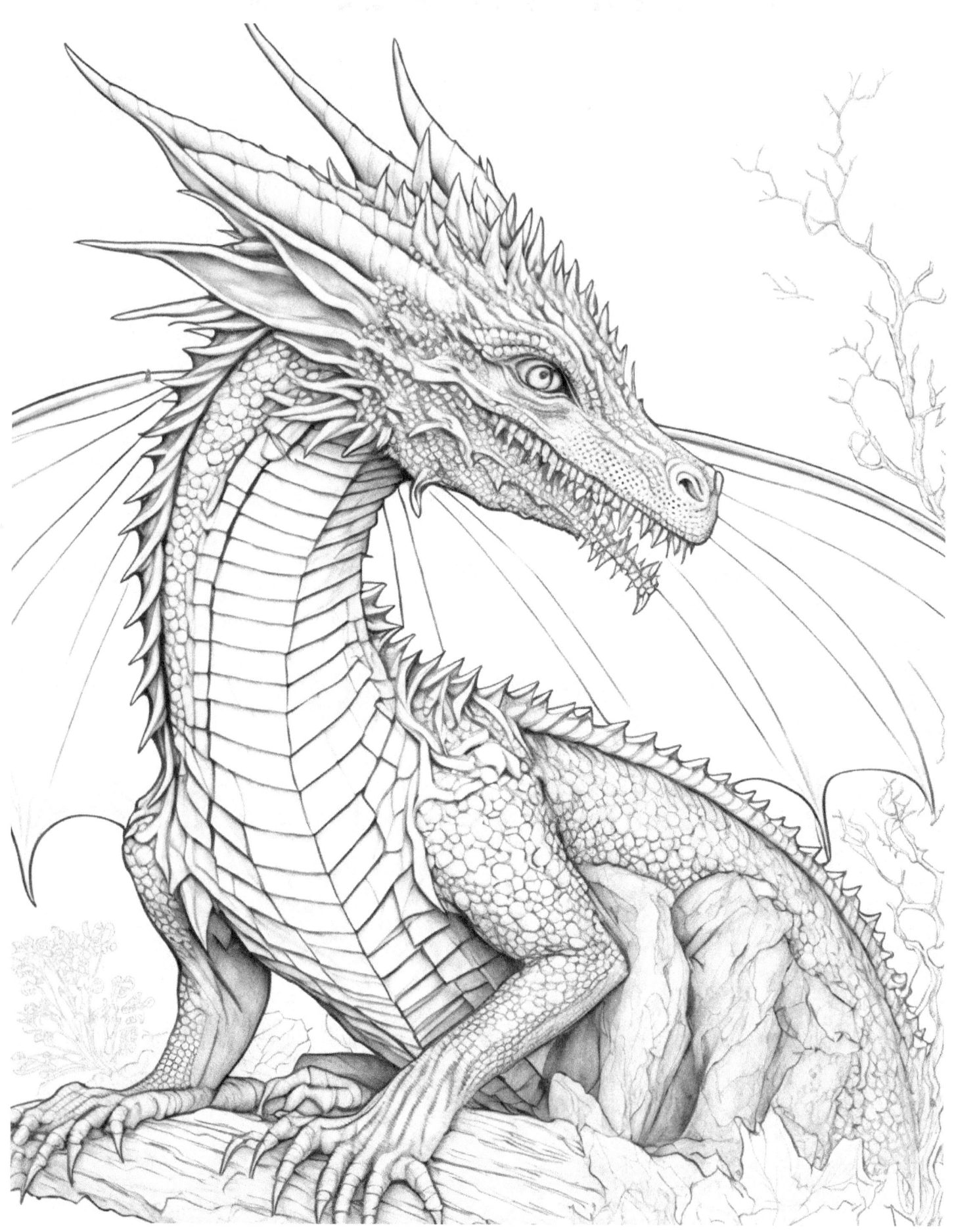

SPYING DRAGONS

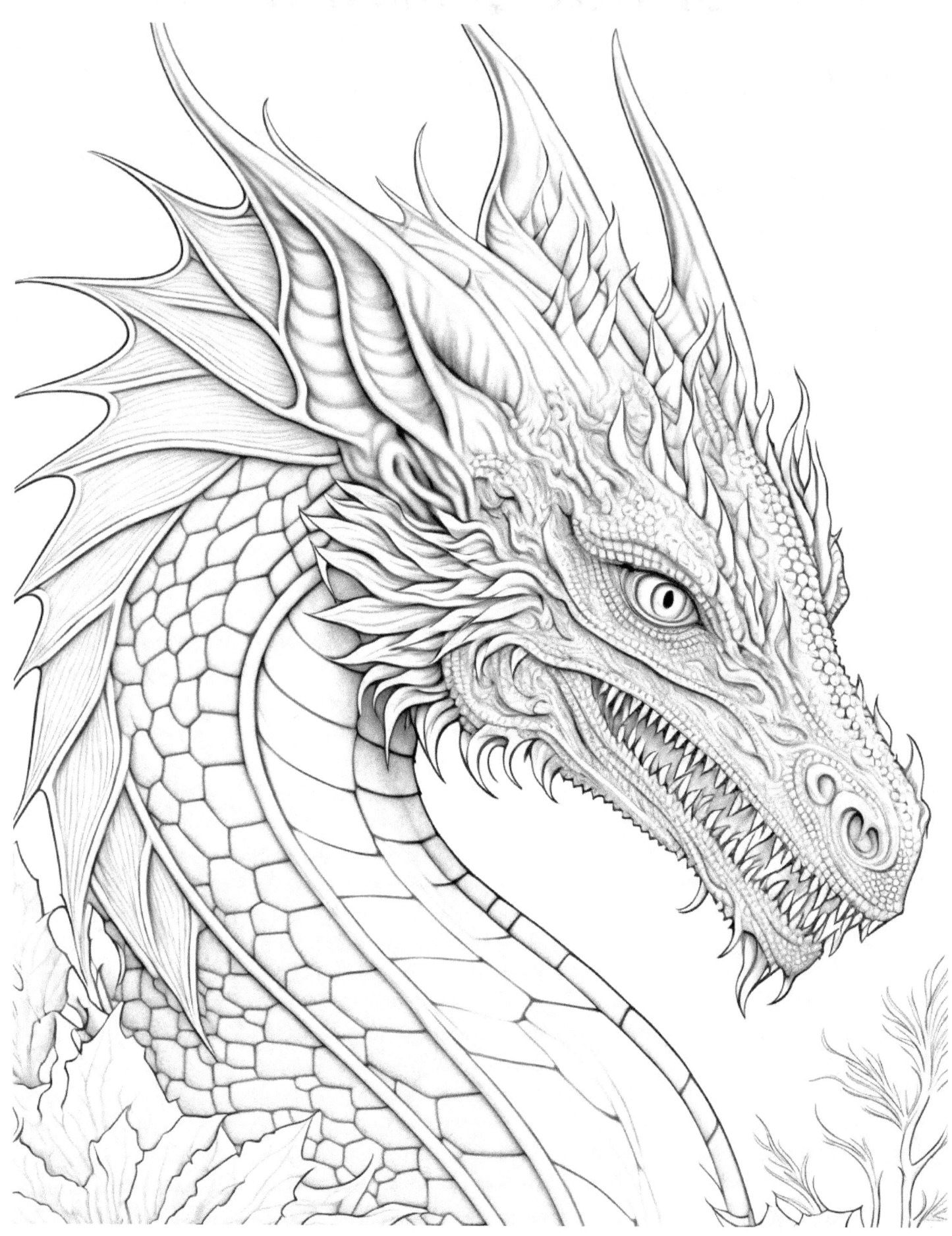

SPYING DRAGONS

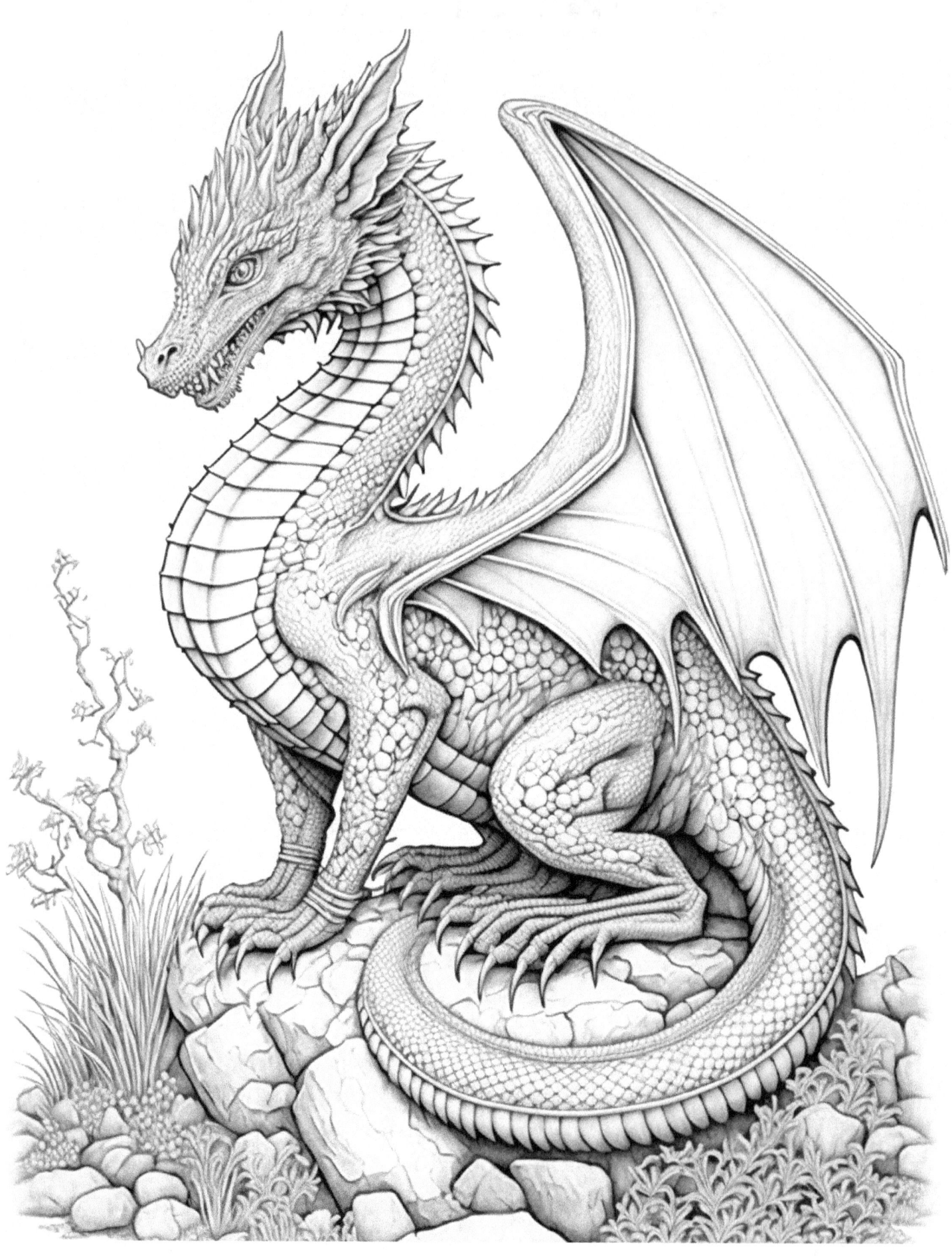

SPYING DRAGONS

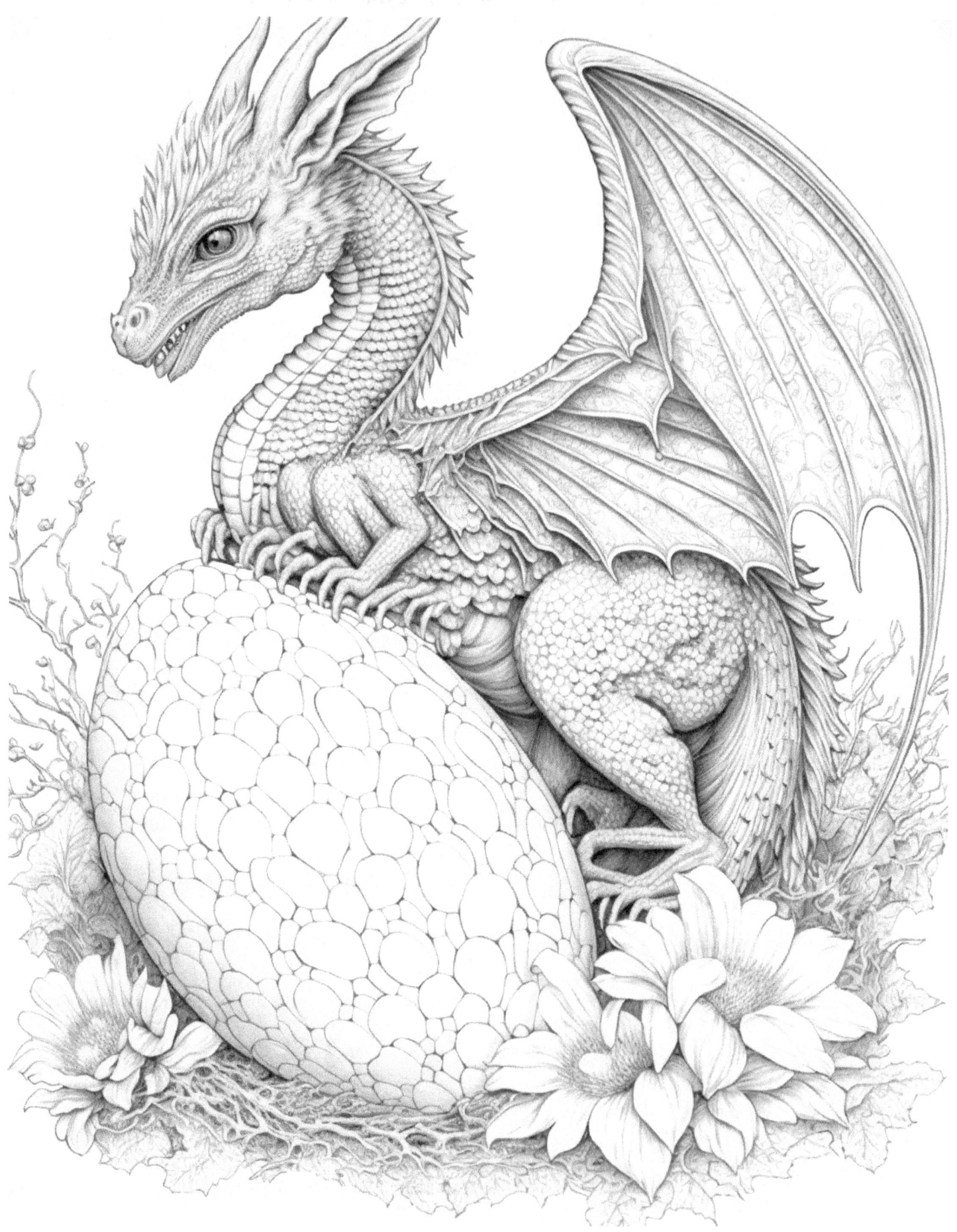

SPYING DRAGONS

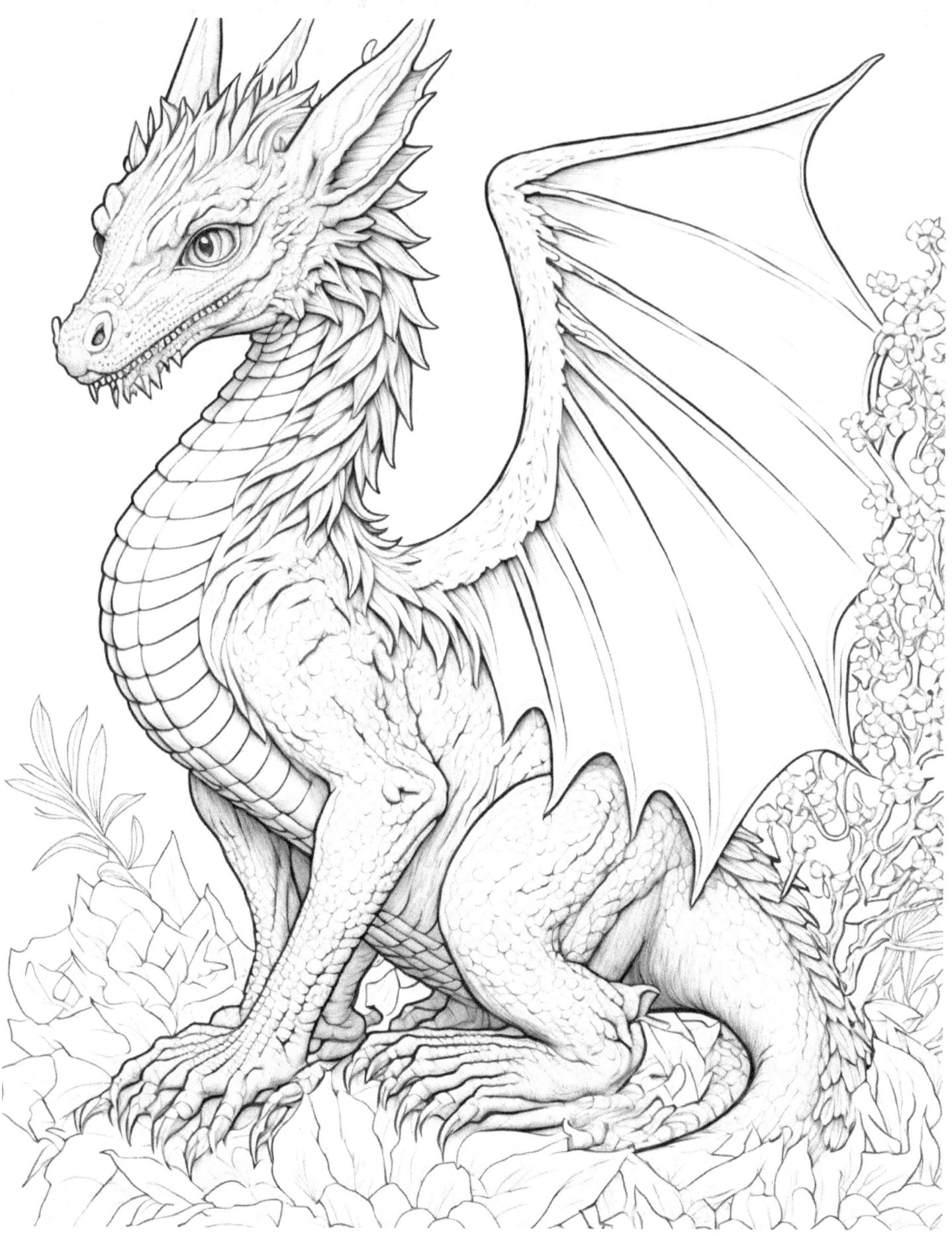

SPYING DRAGONS

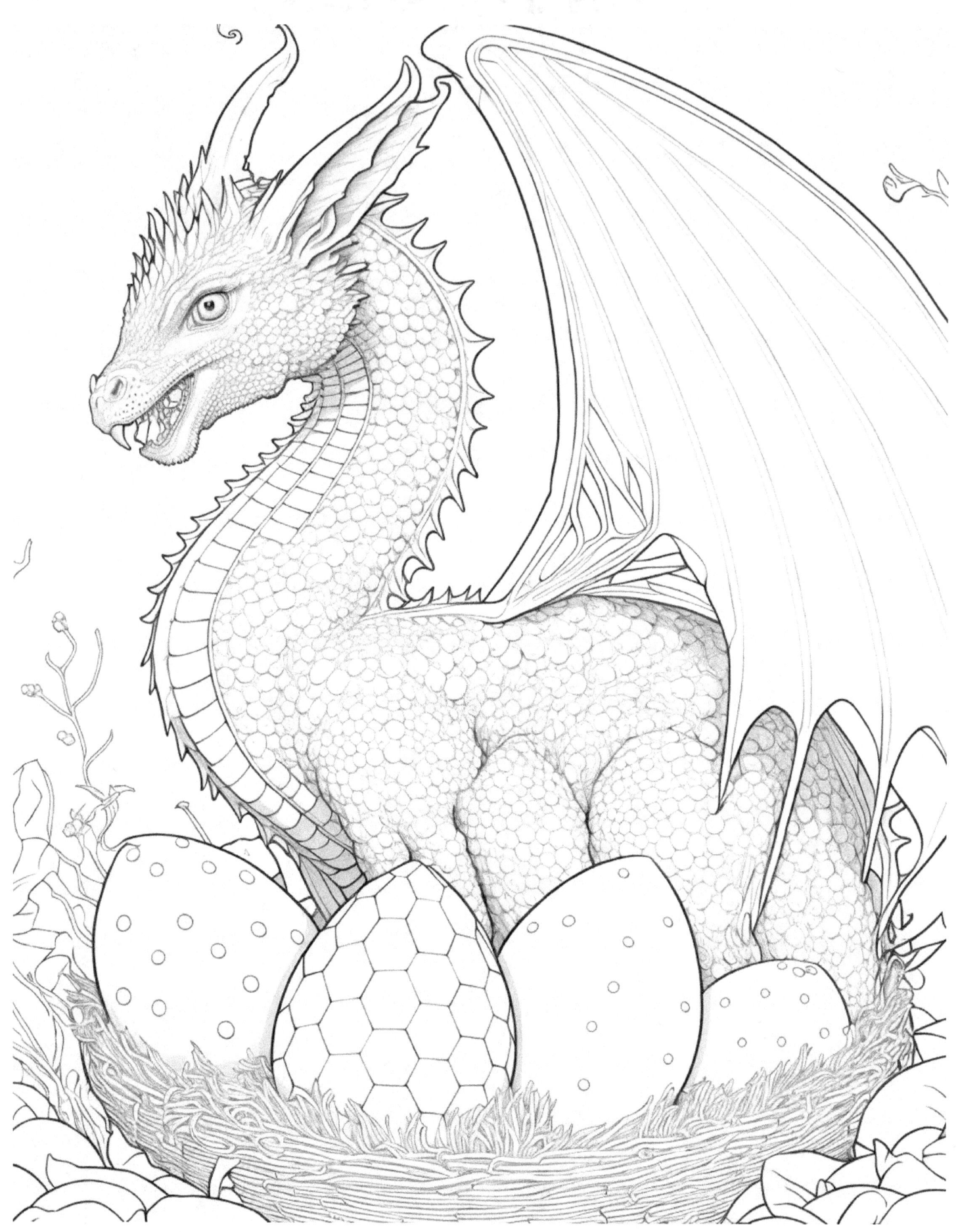

SPYING DRAGONS

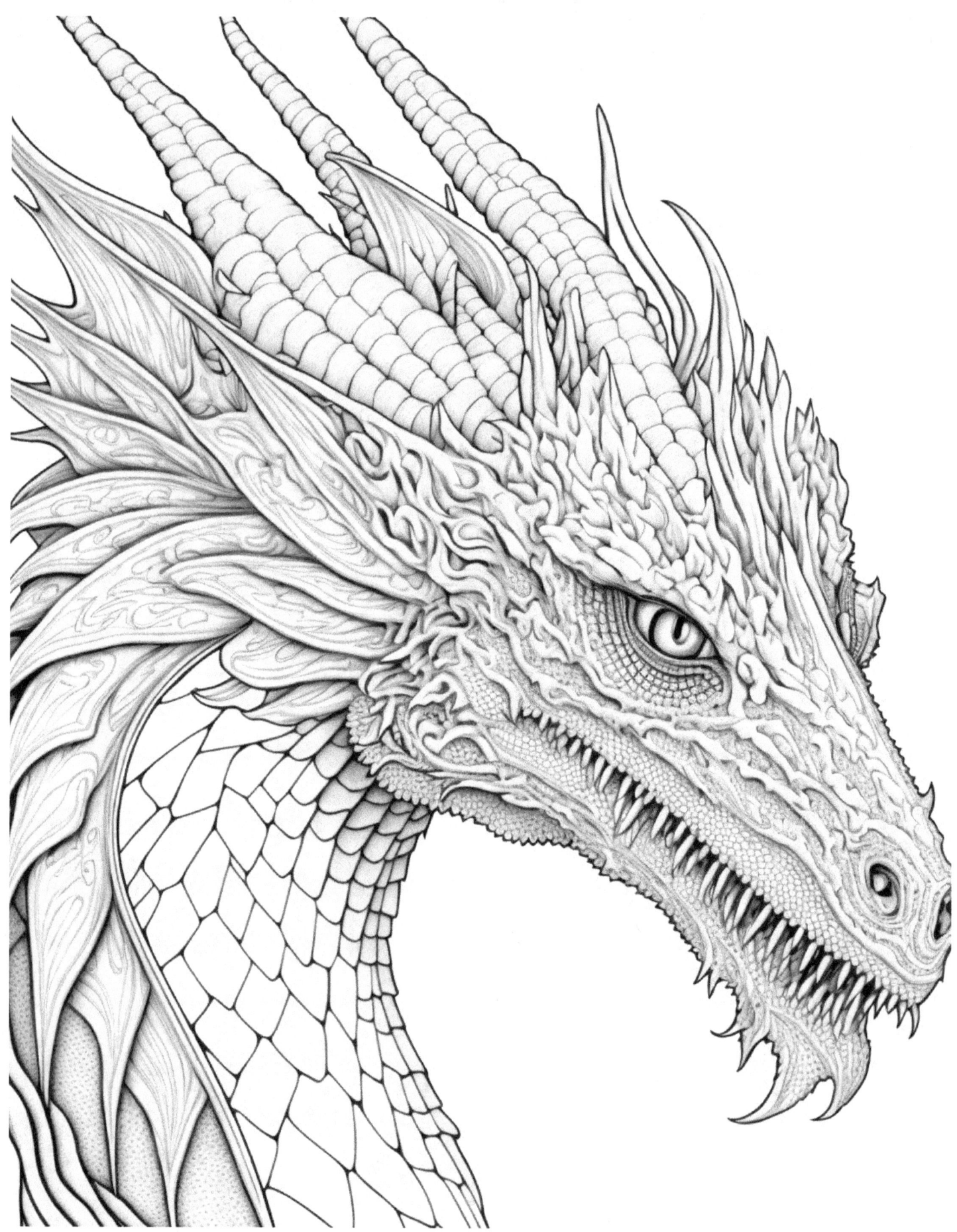

SPYING DRAGONS

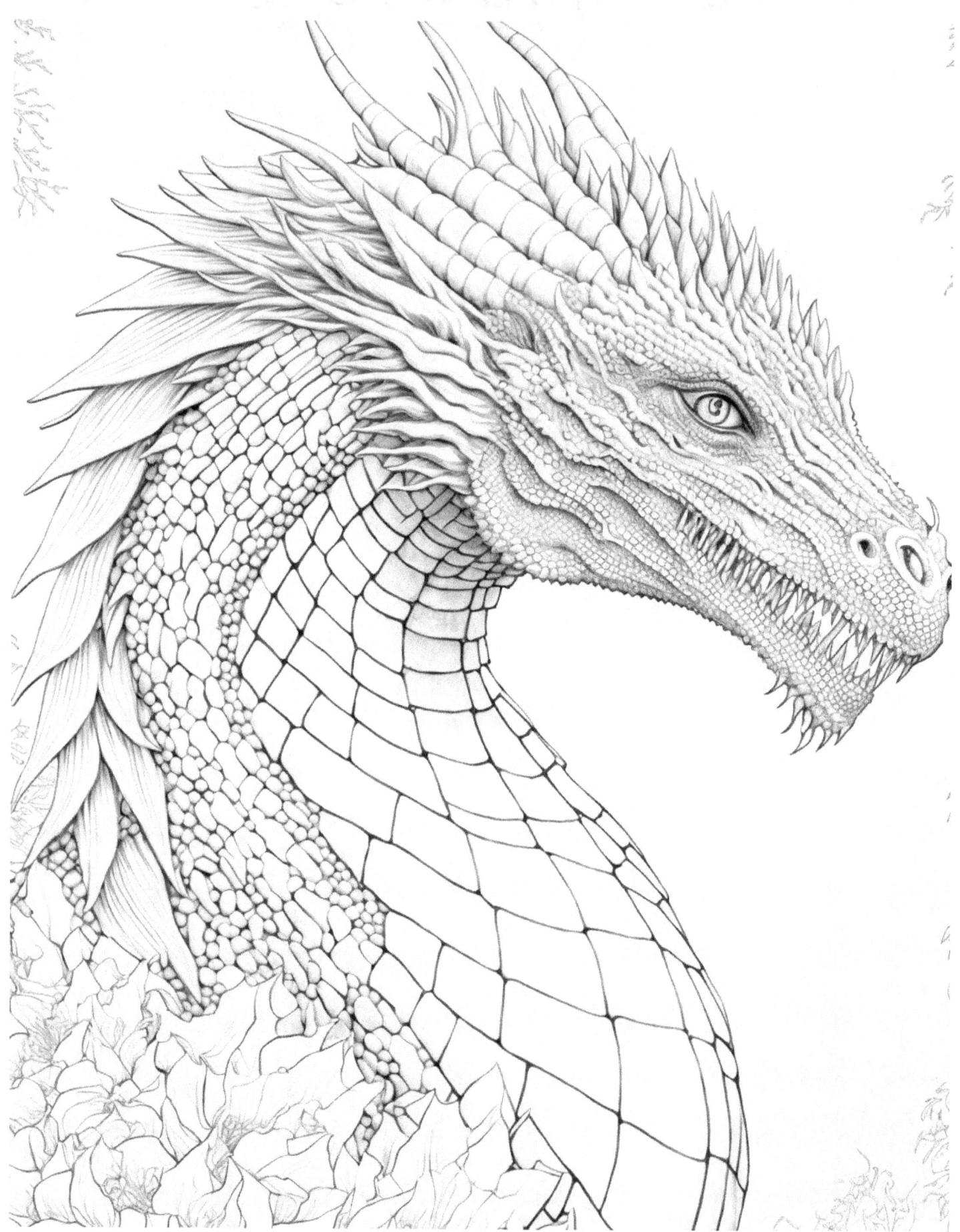

SPYING DRAGONS

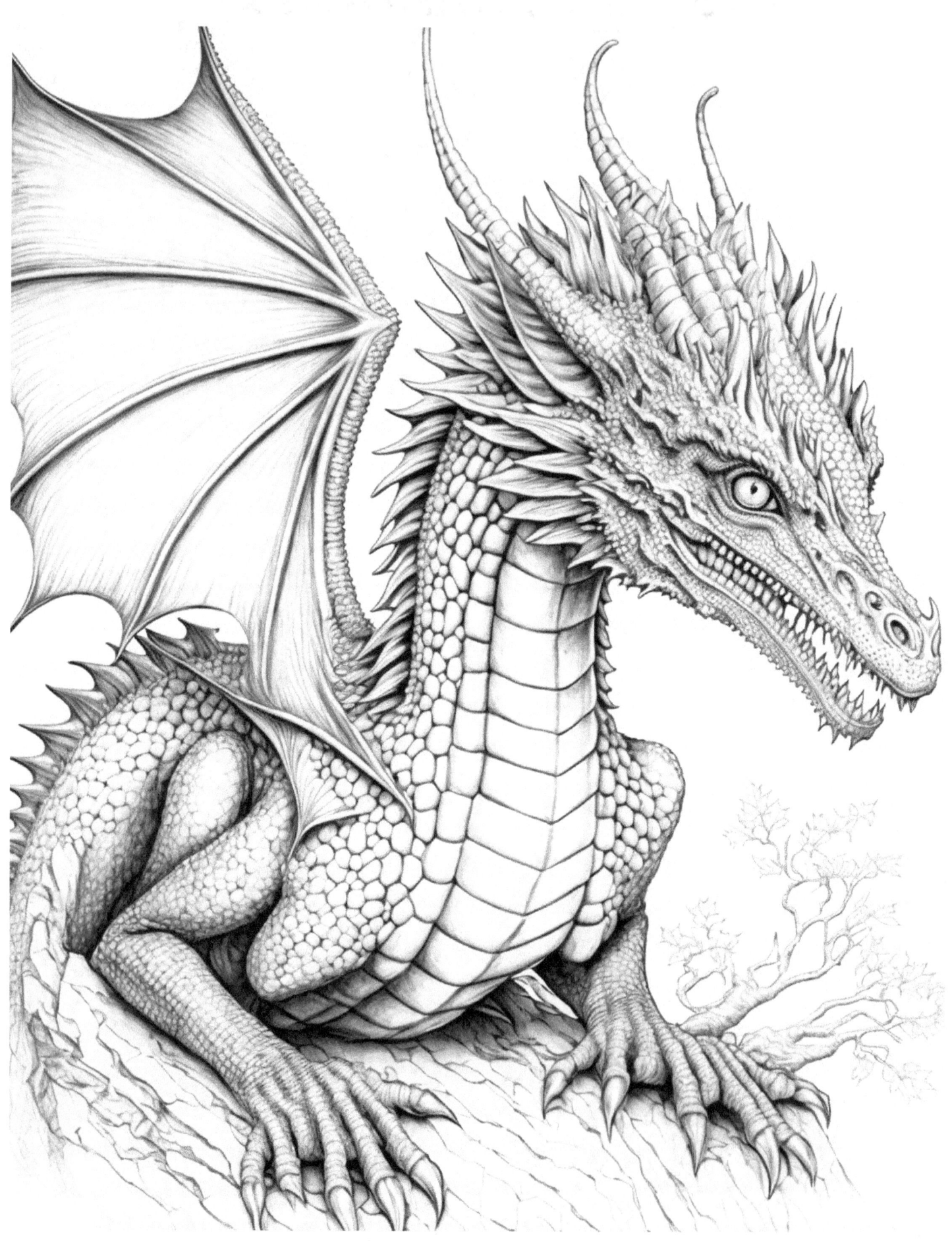

SPYING DRAGONS

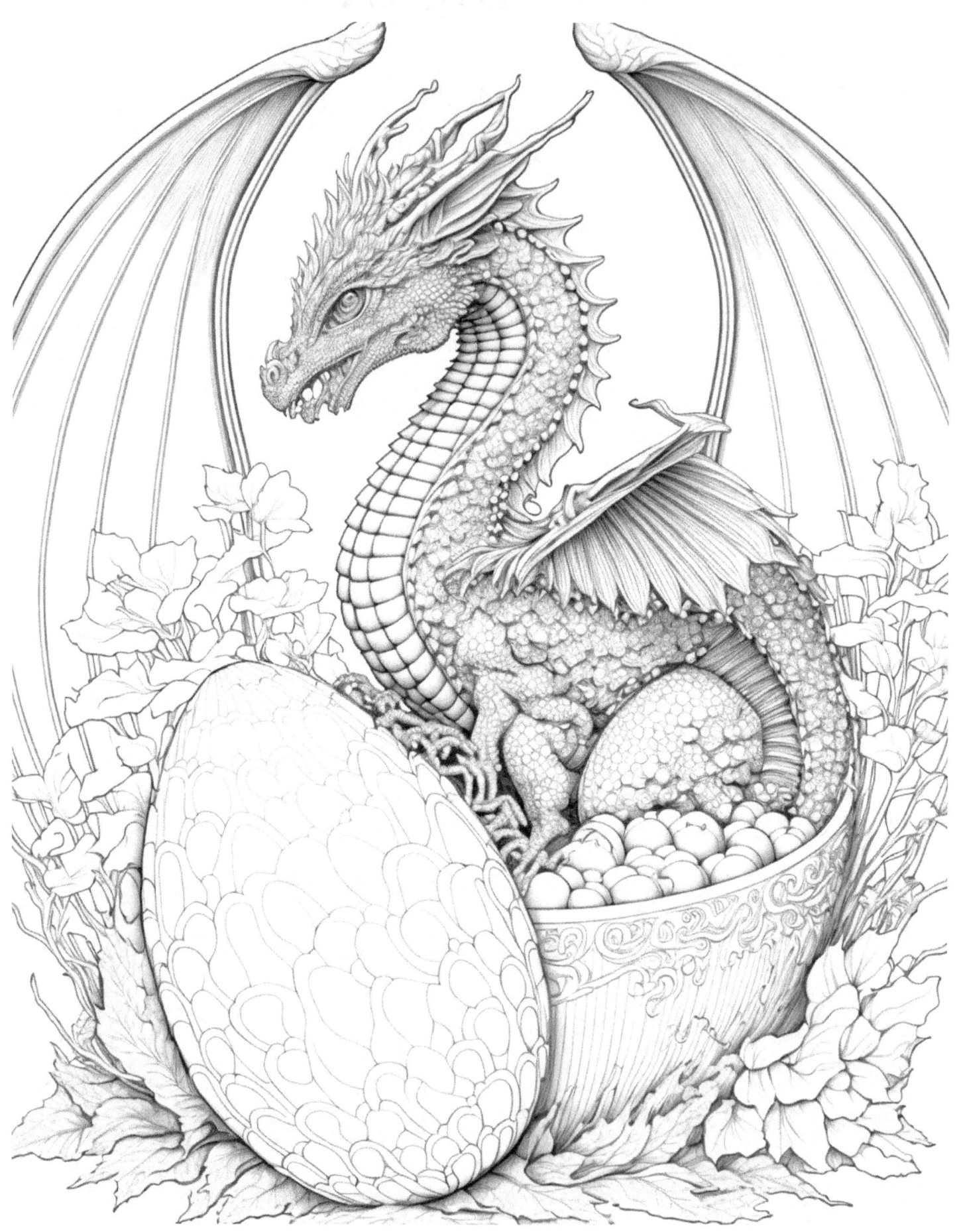

SPYING DRAGONS

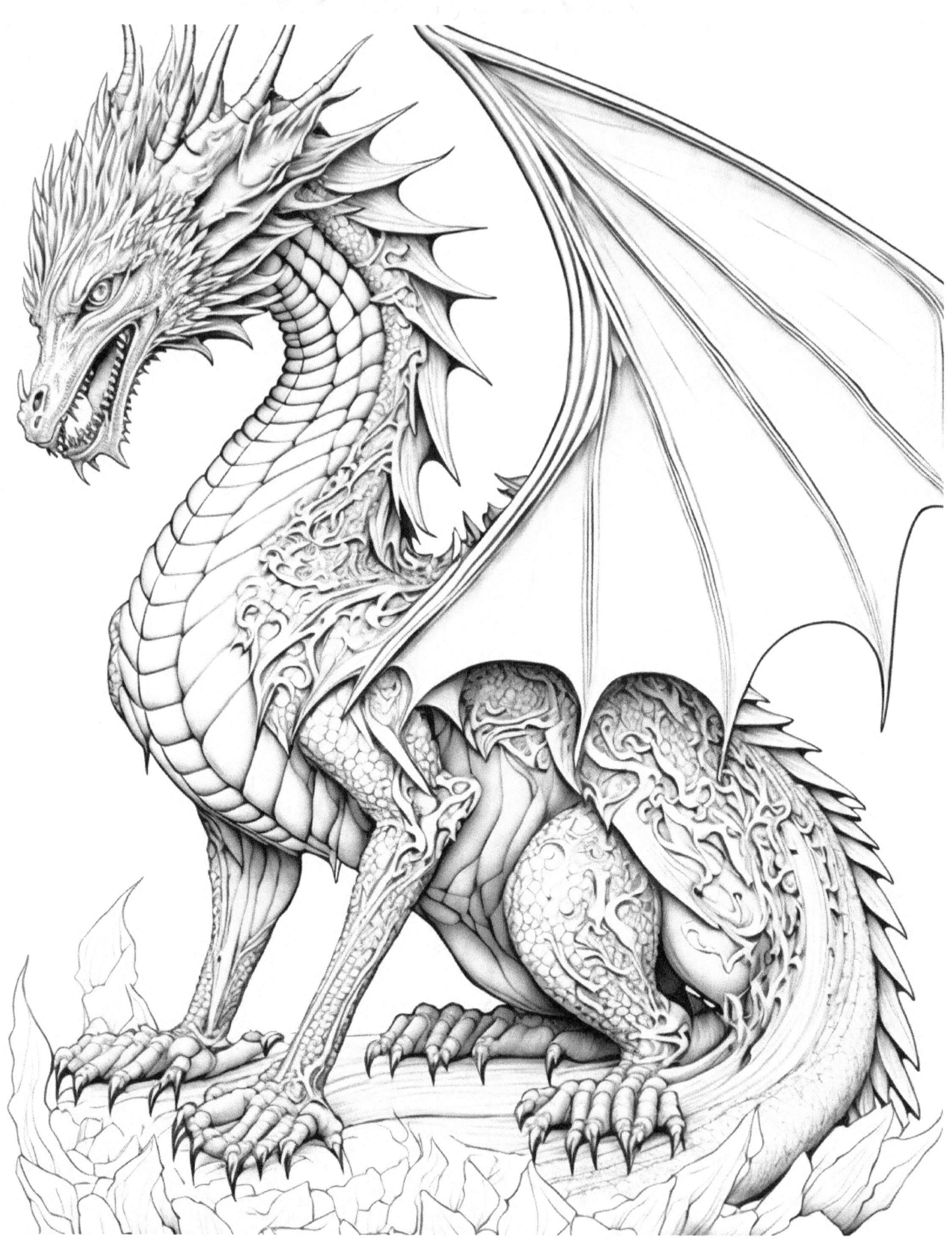

SPYING DRAGONS

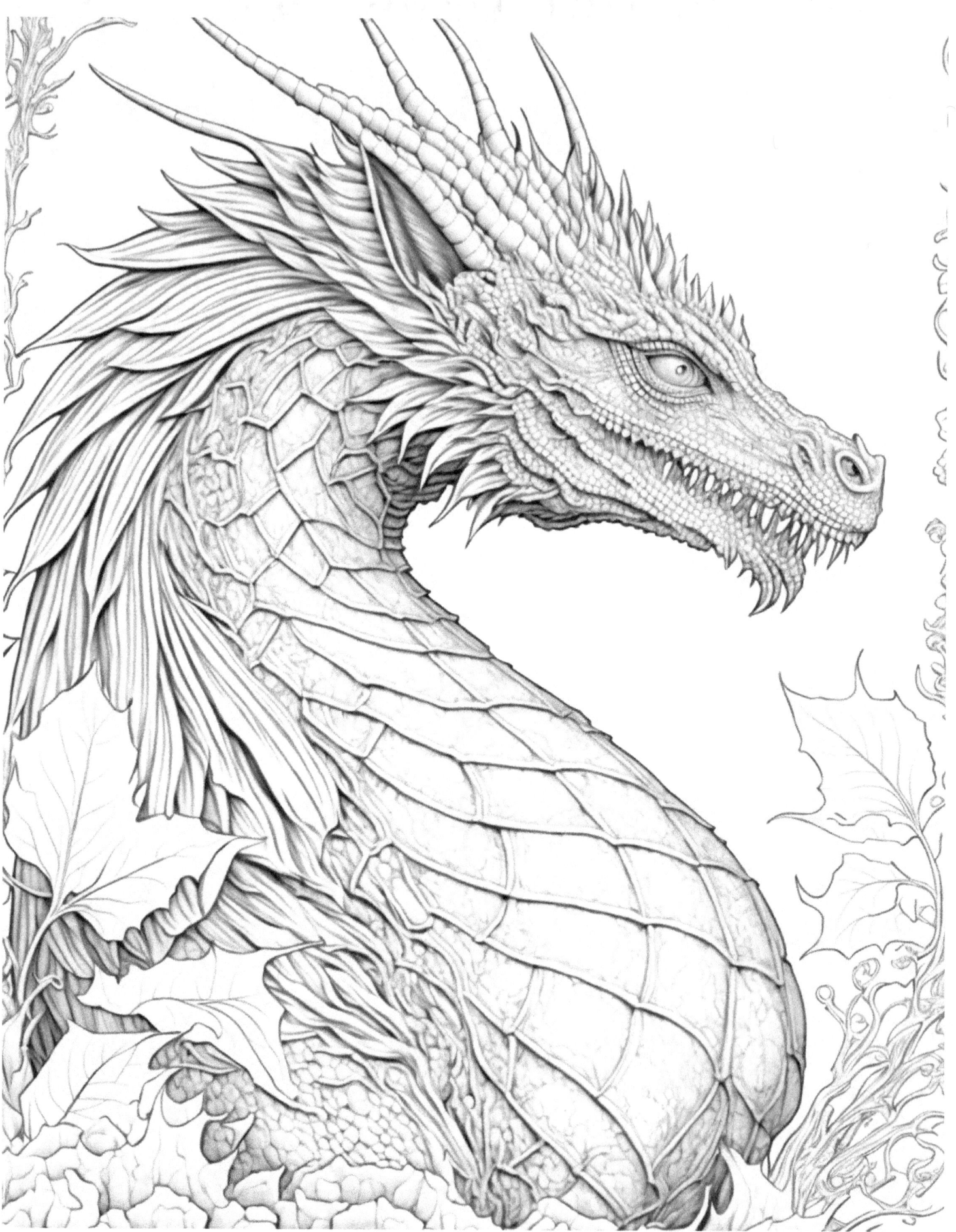

SPYING DRAGONS

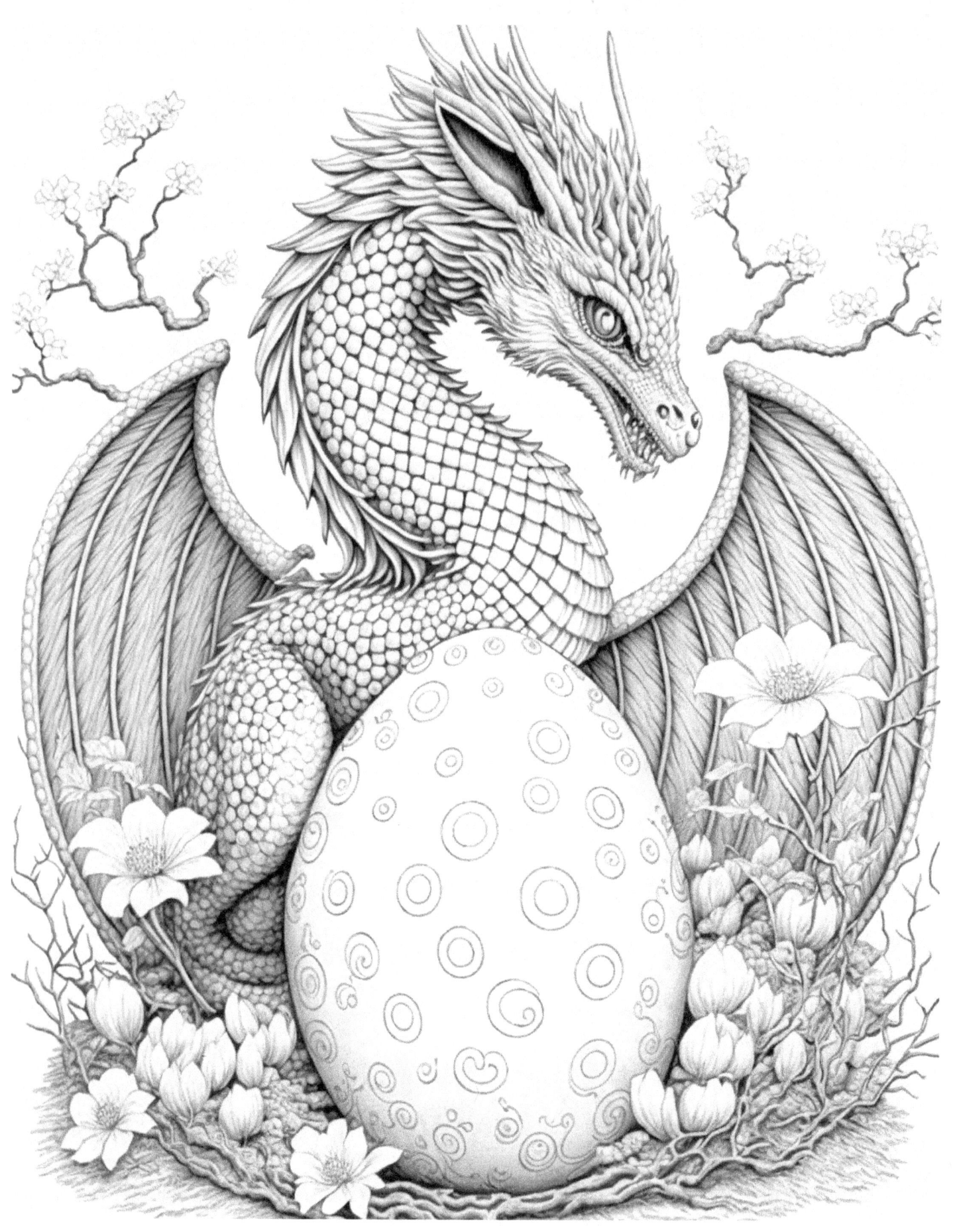

SPYING DRAGONS

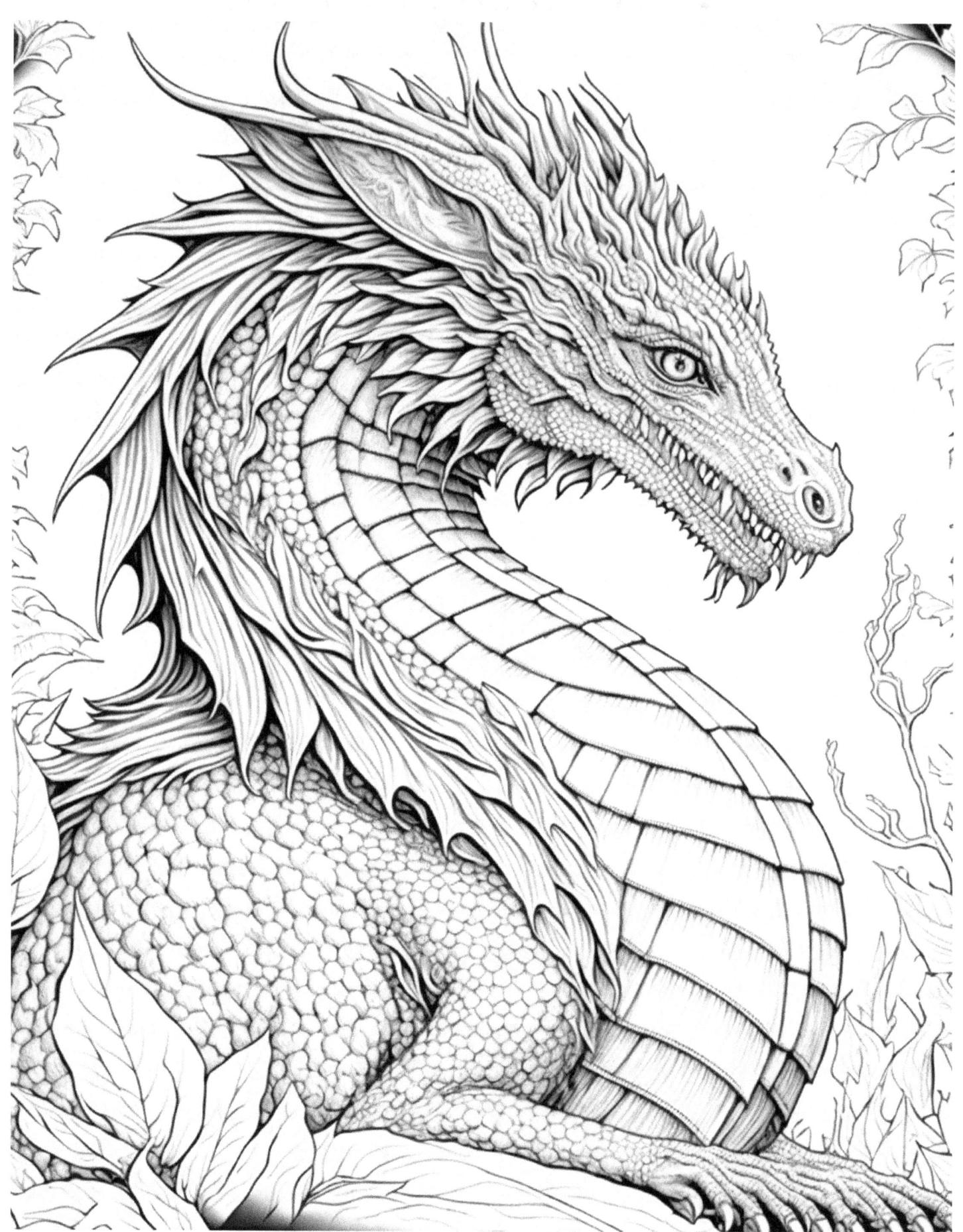

SPYING DRAGONS

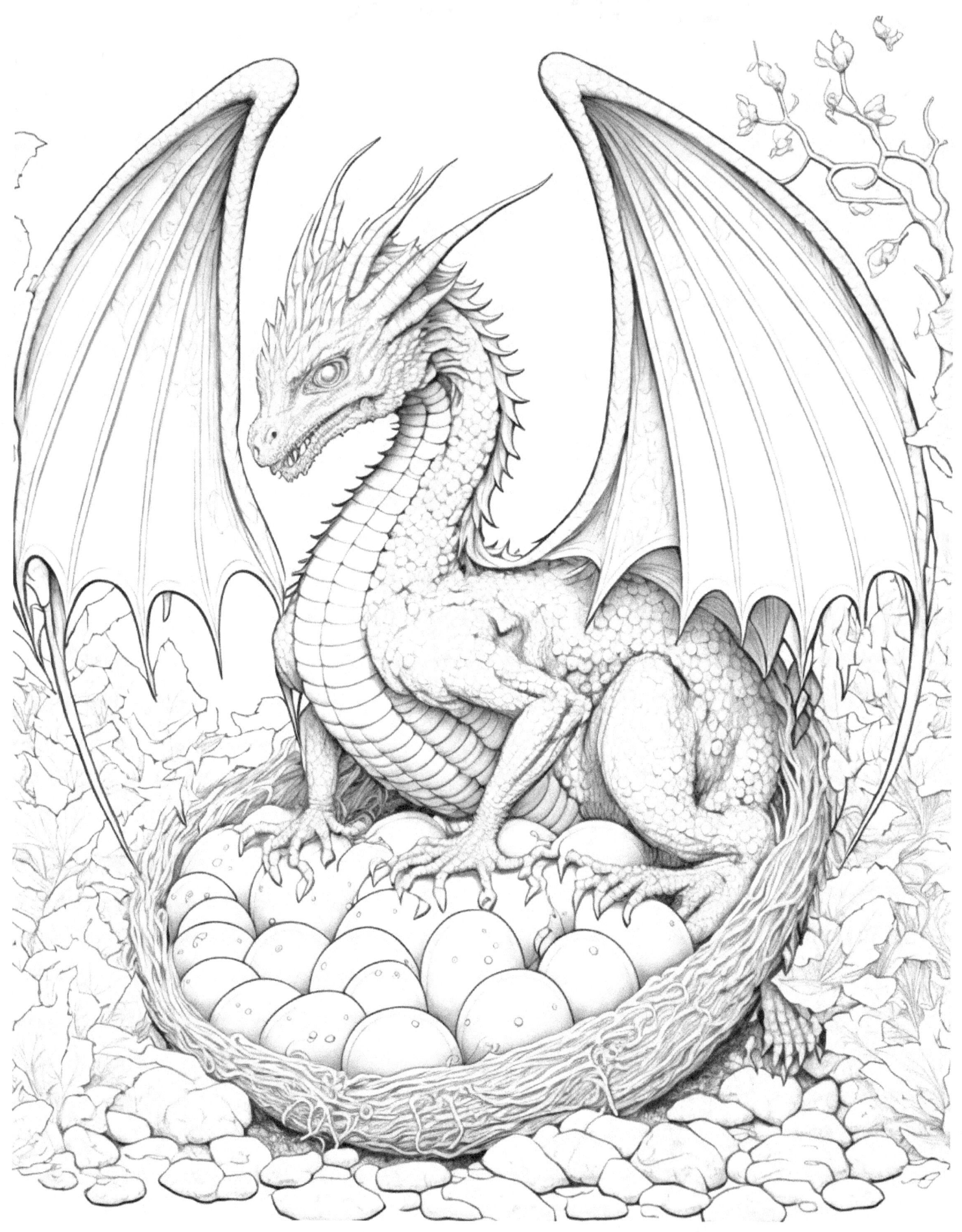

SPYING DRAGONS

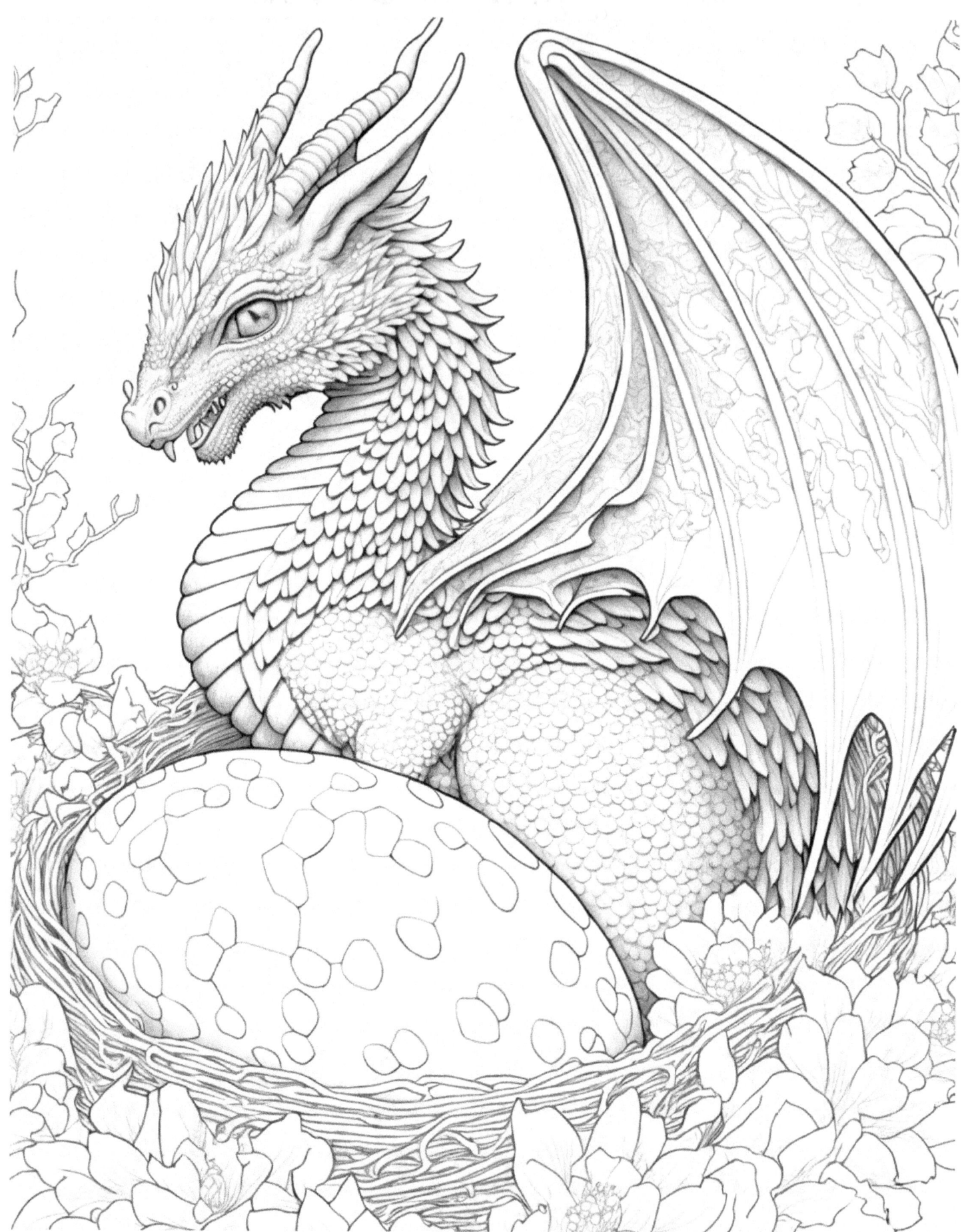

SPYING DRAGONS

SPYING DRAGONS

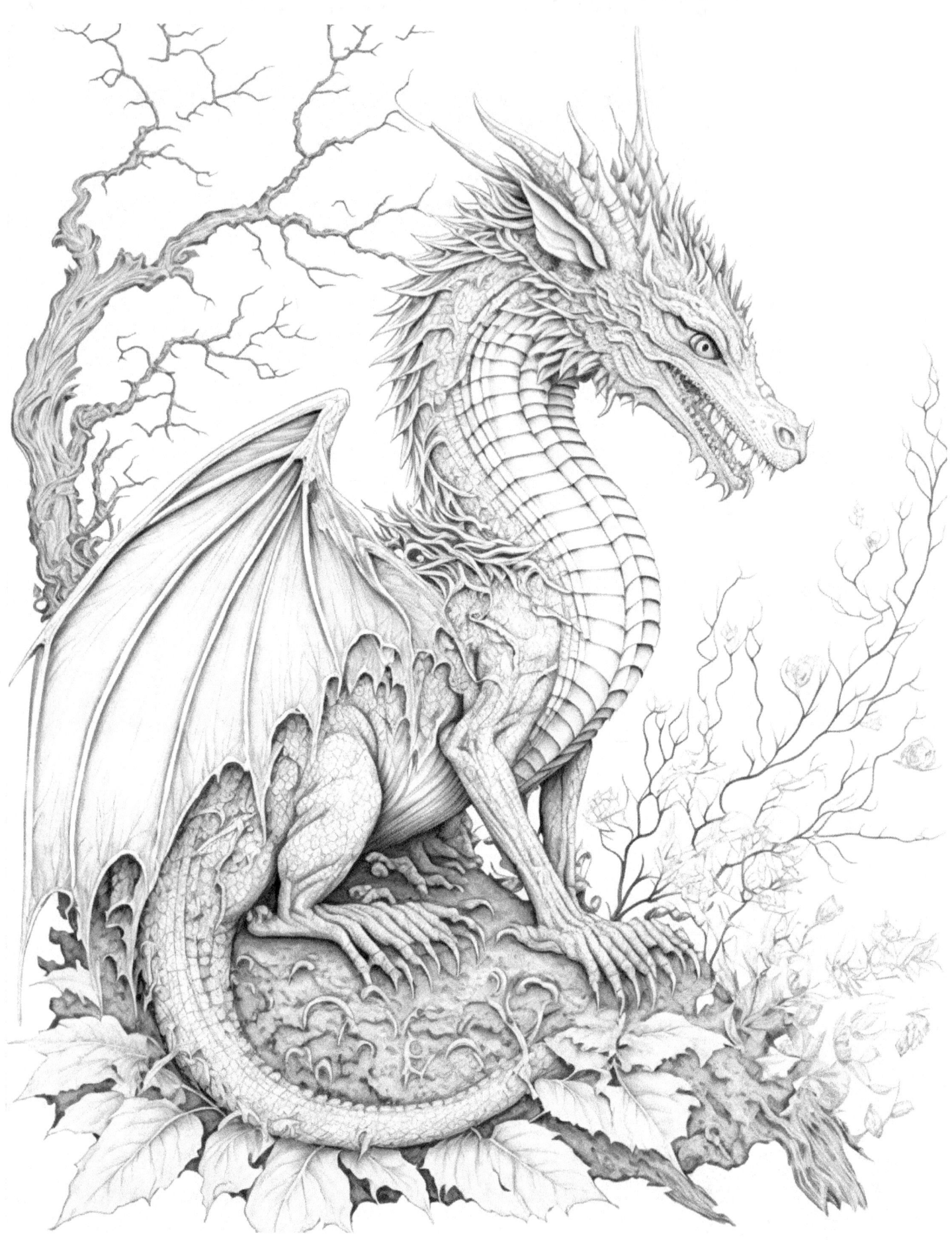

SPYING DRAGONS

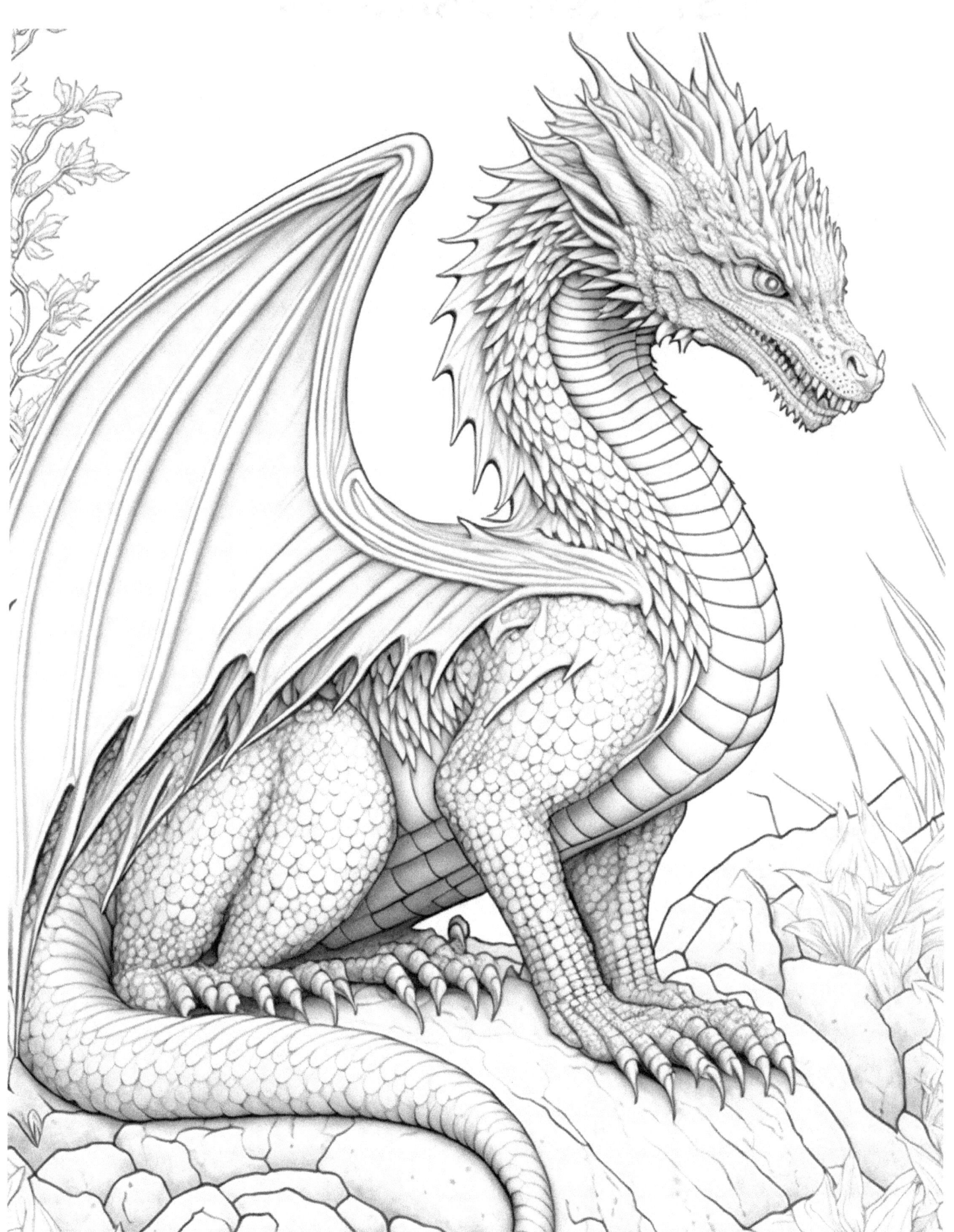

SPYING DRAGONS

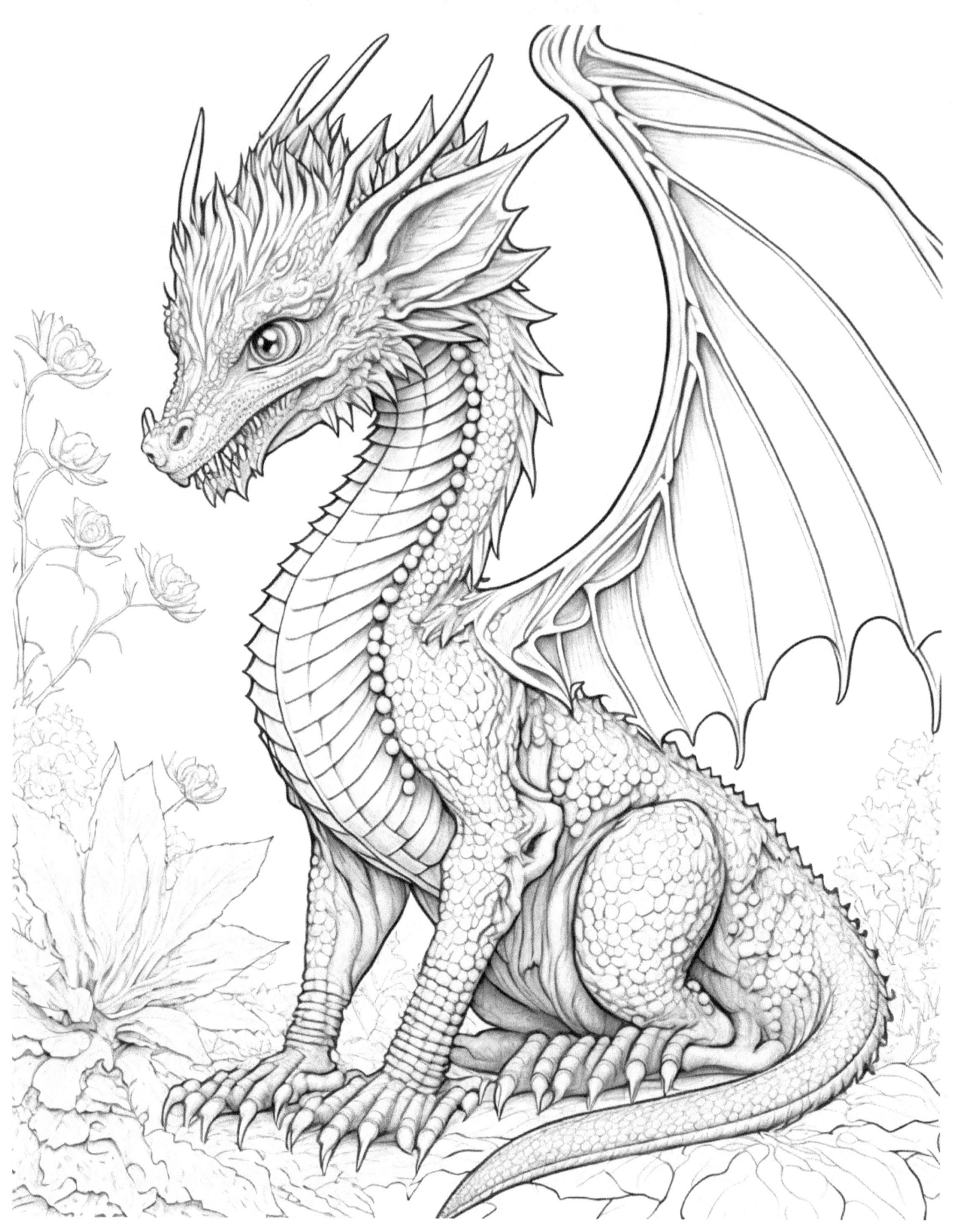

SPYING DRAGONS

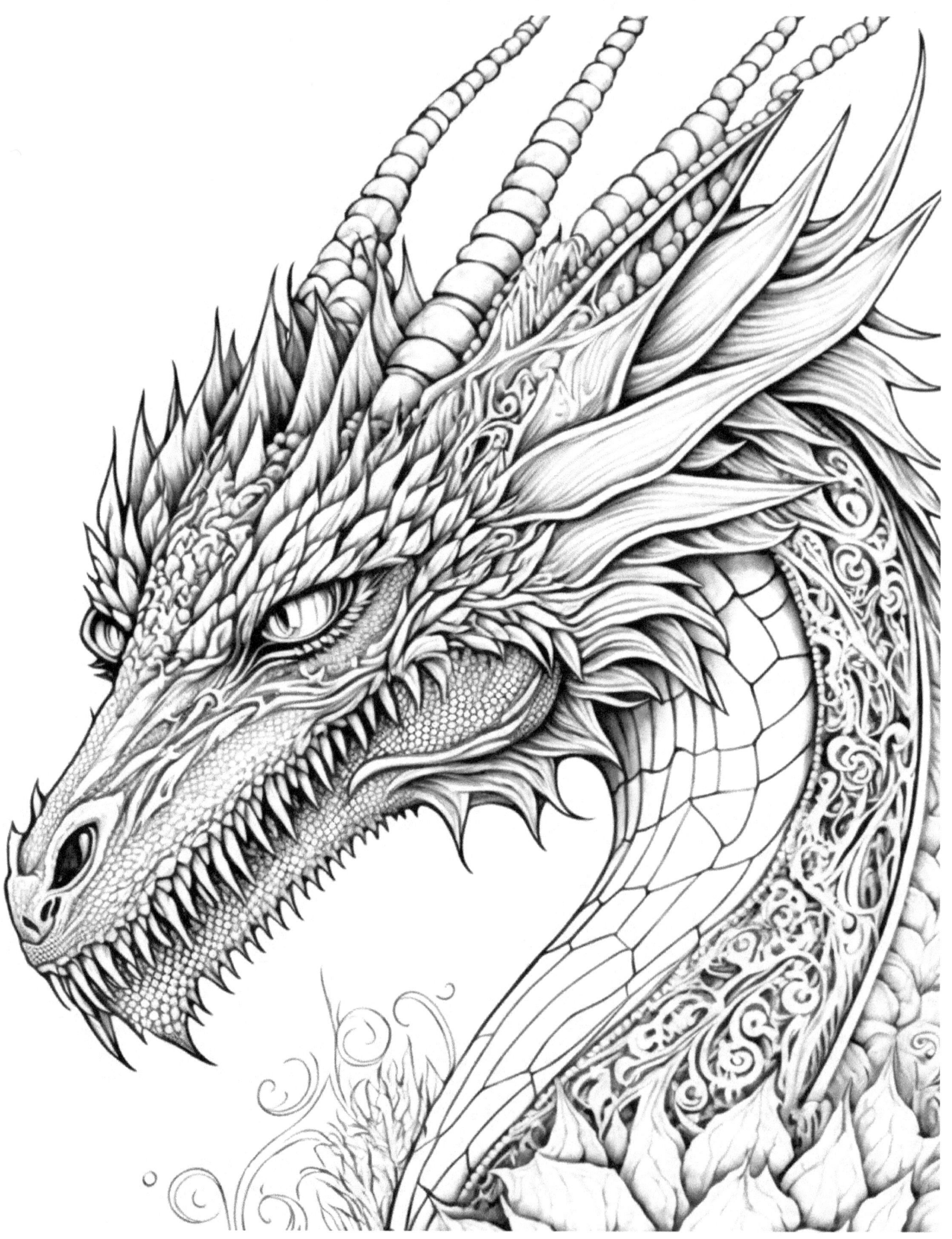

SPYING DRAGONS

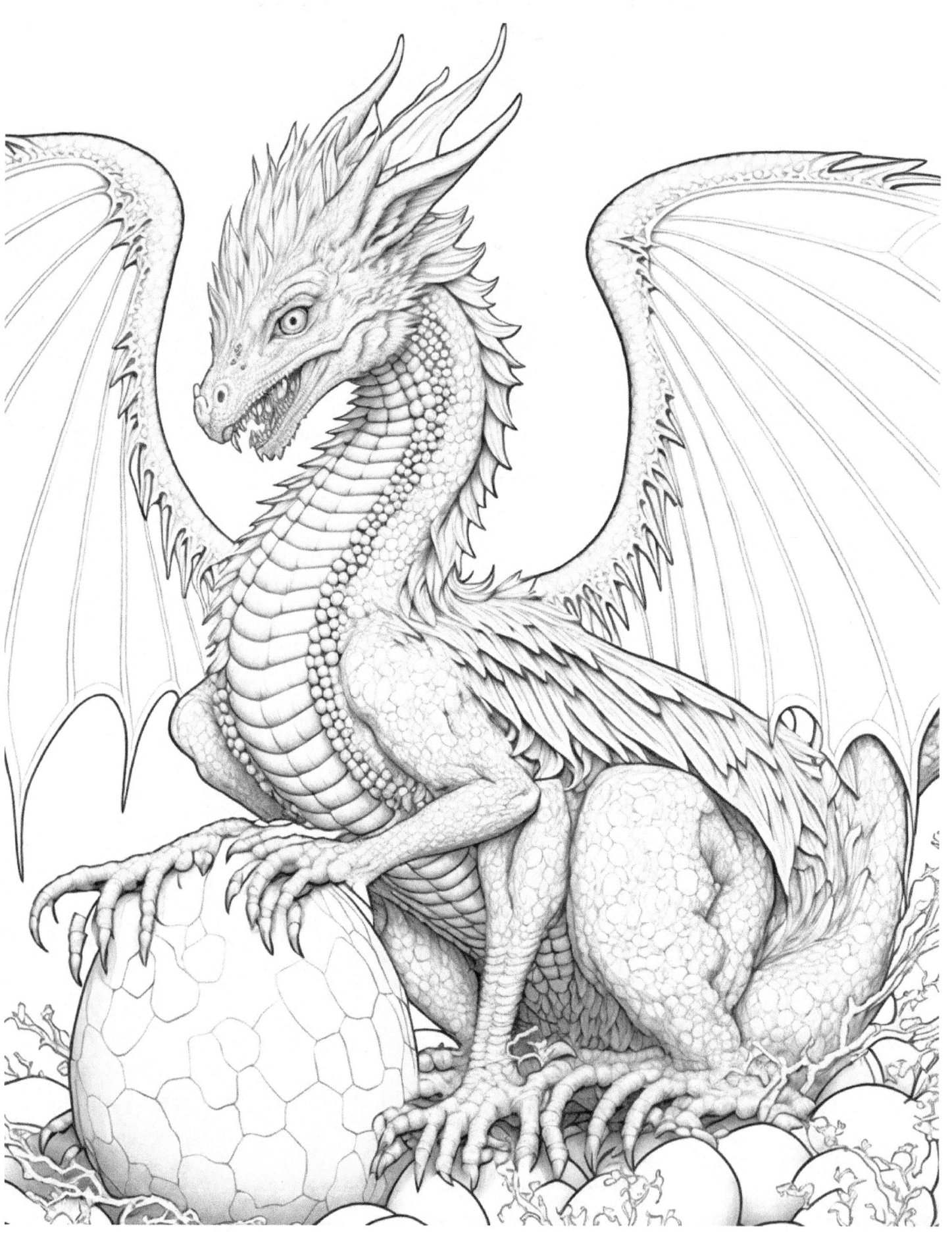

SPYING DRAGONS

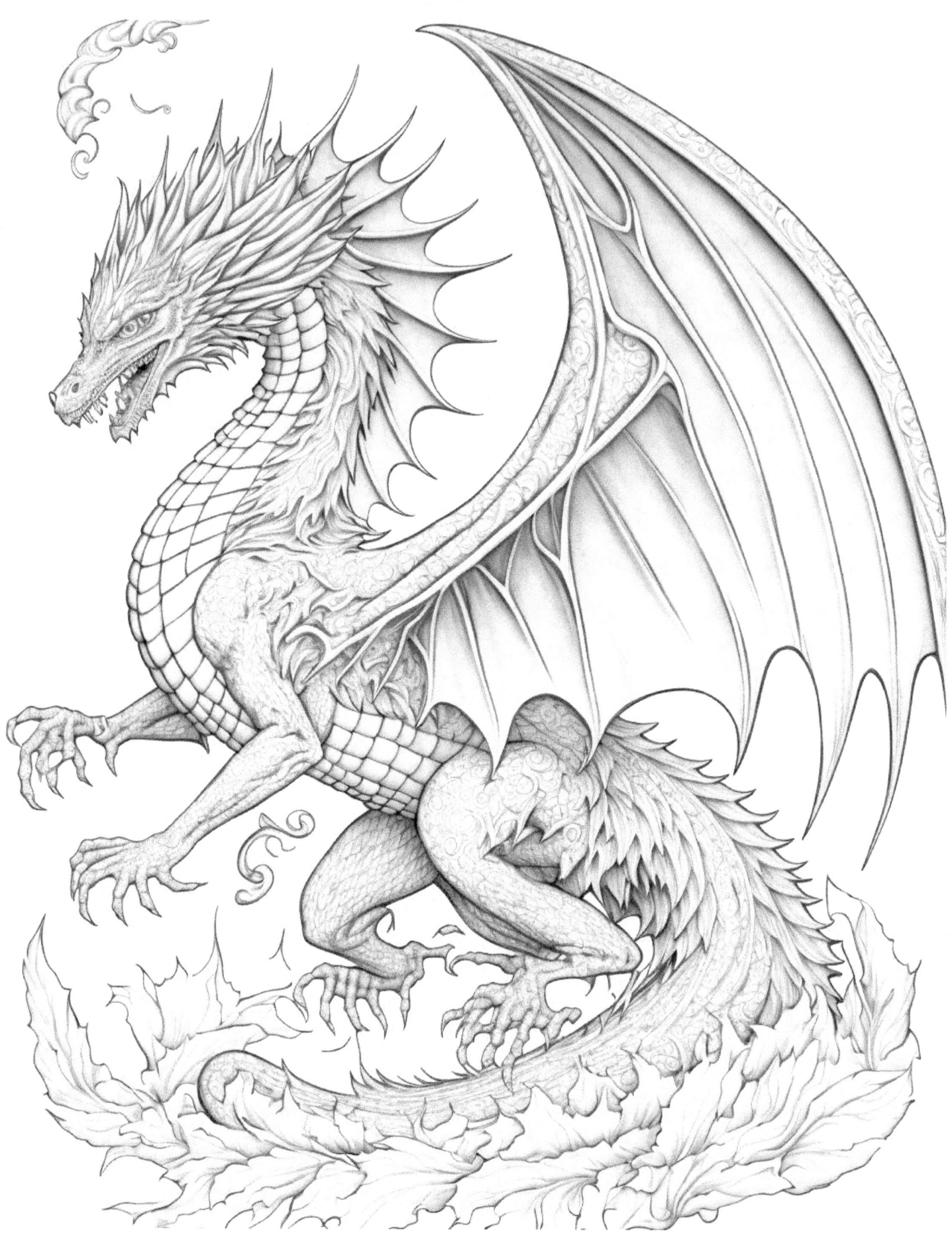

SPYING DRAGONS

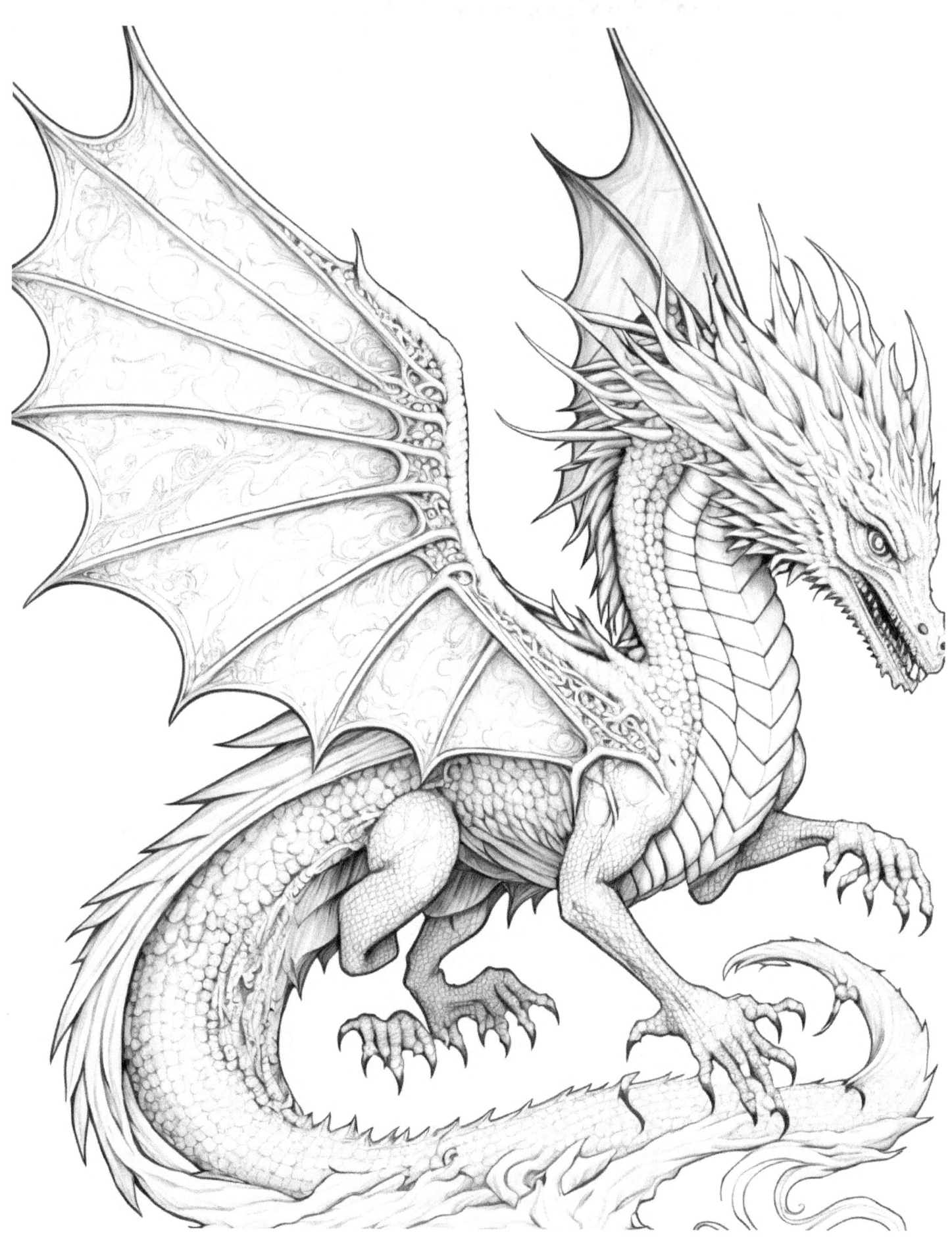

SPYING DRAGONS

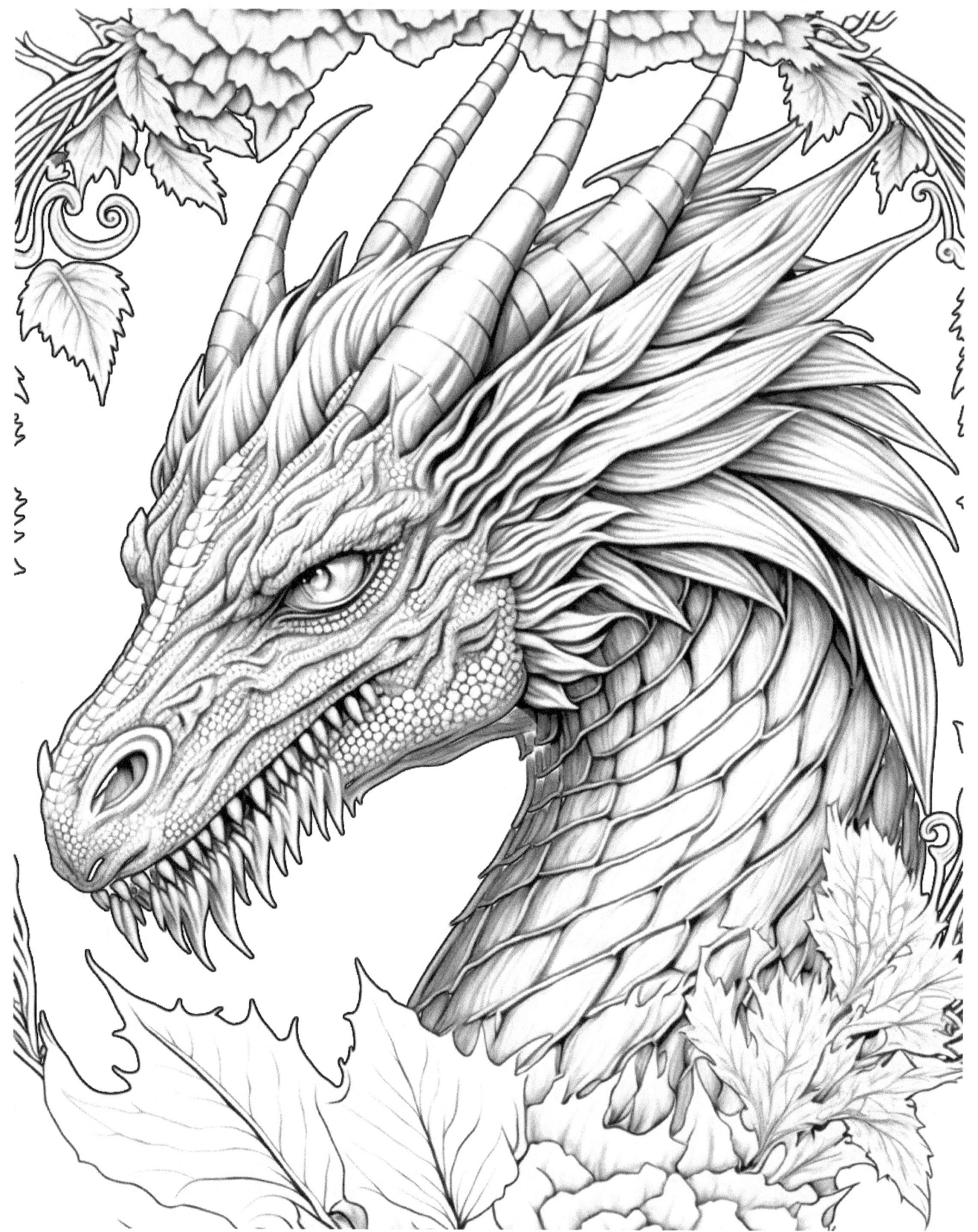

SPYING DRAGONS

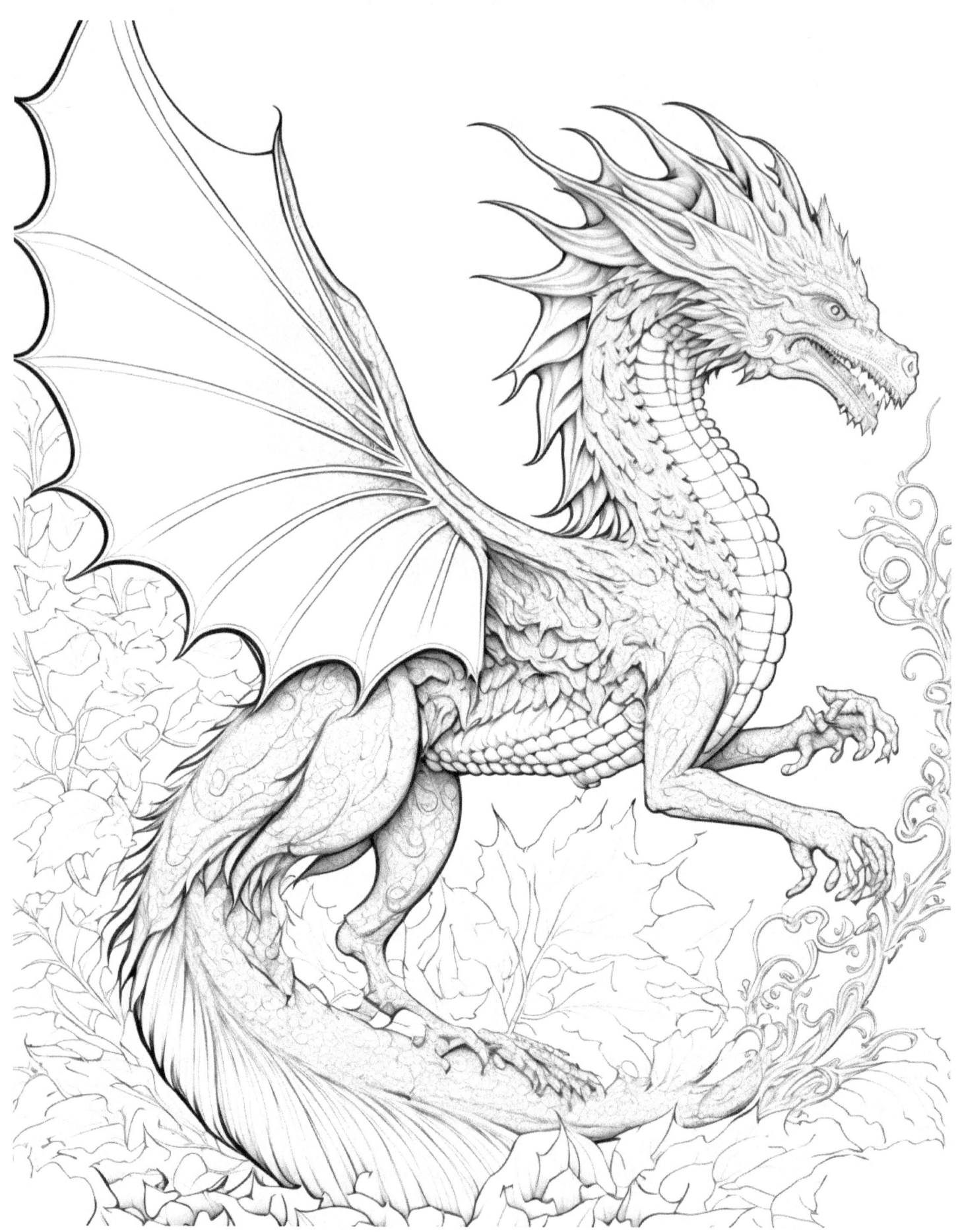

SPYING DRAGONS

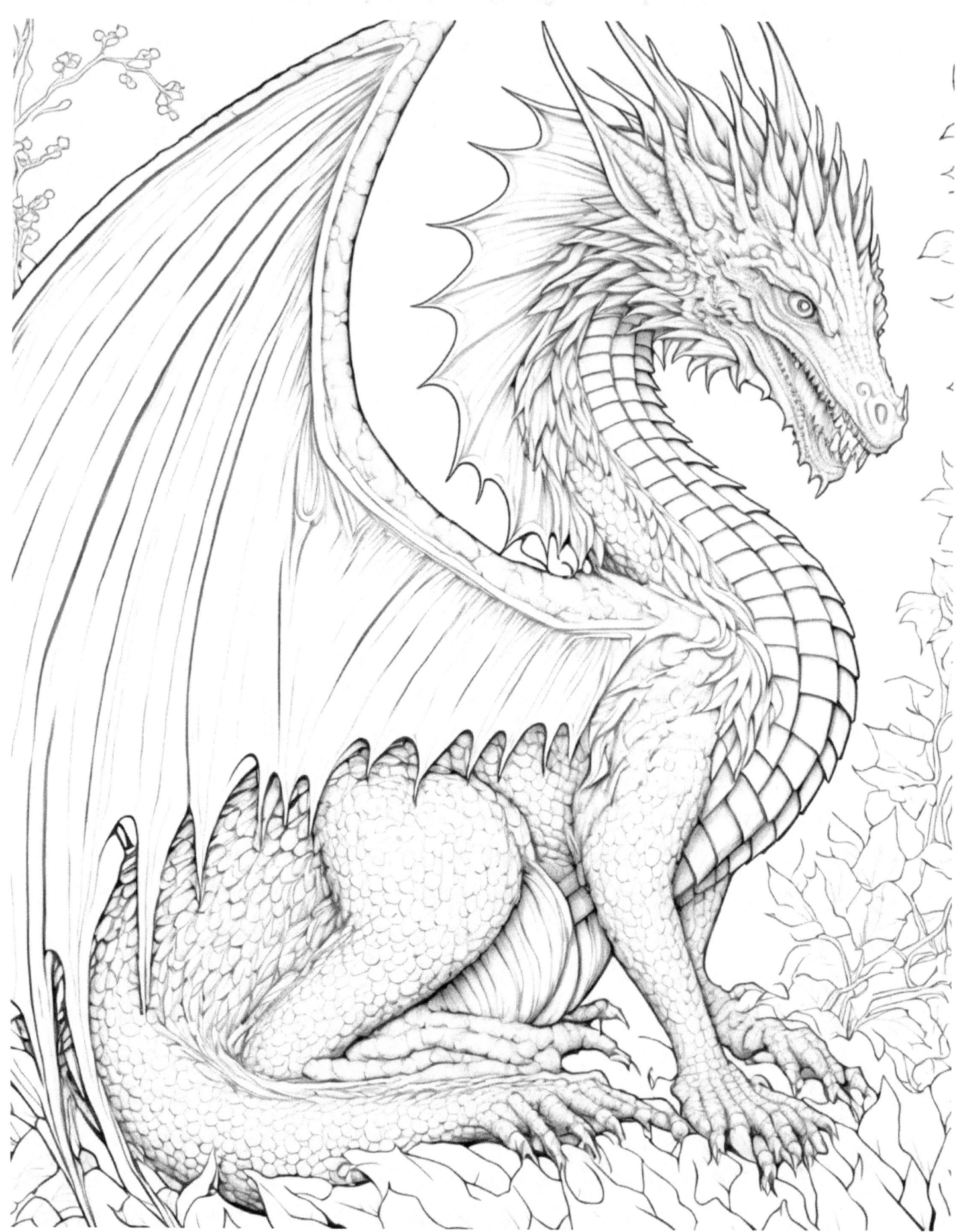

SPYING DRAGONS

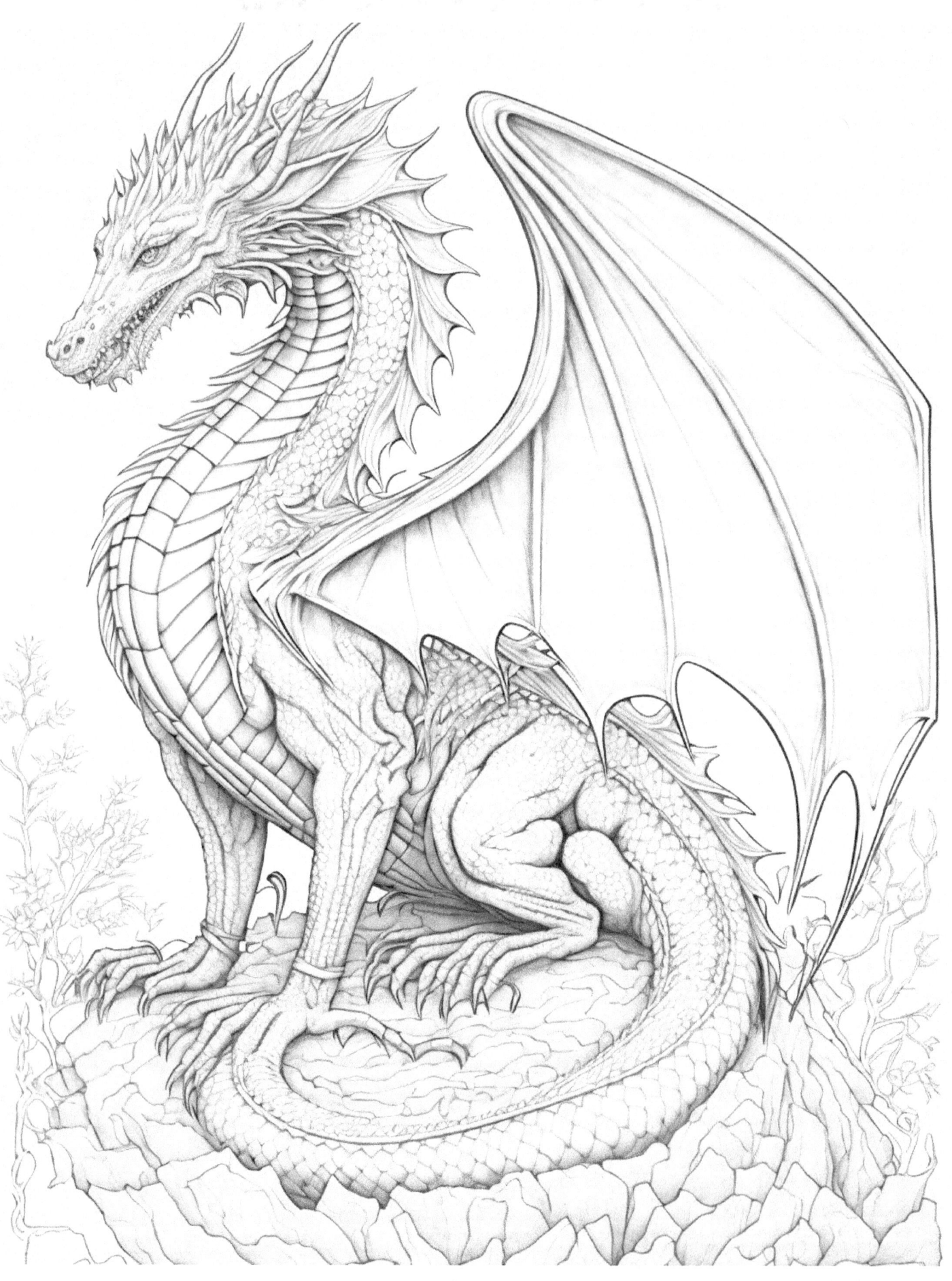

SPYING DRAGONS

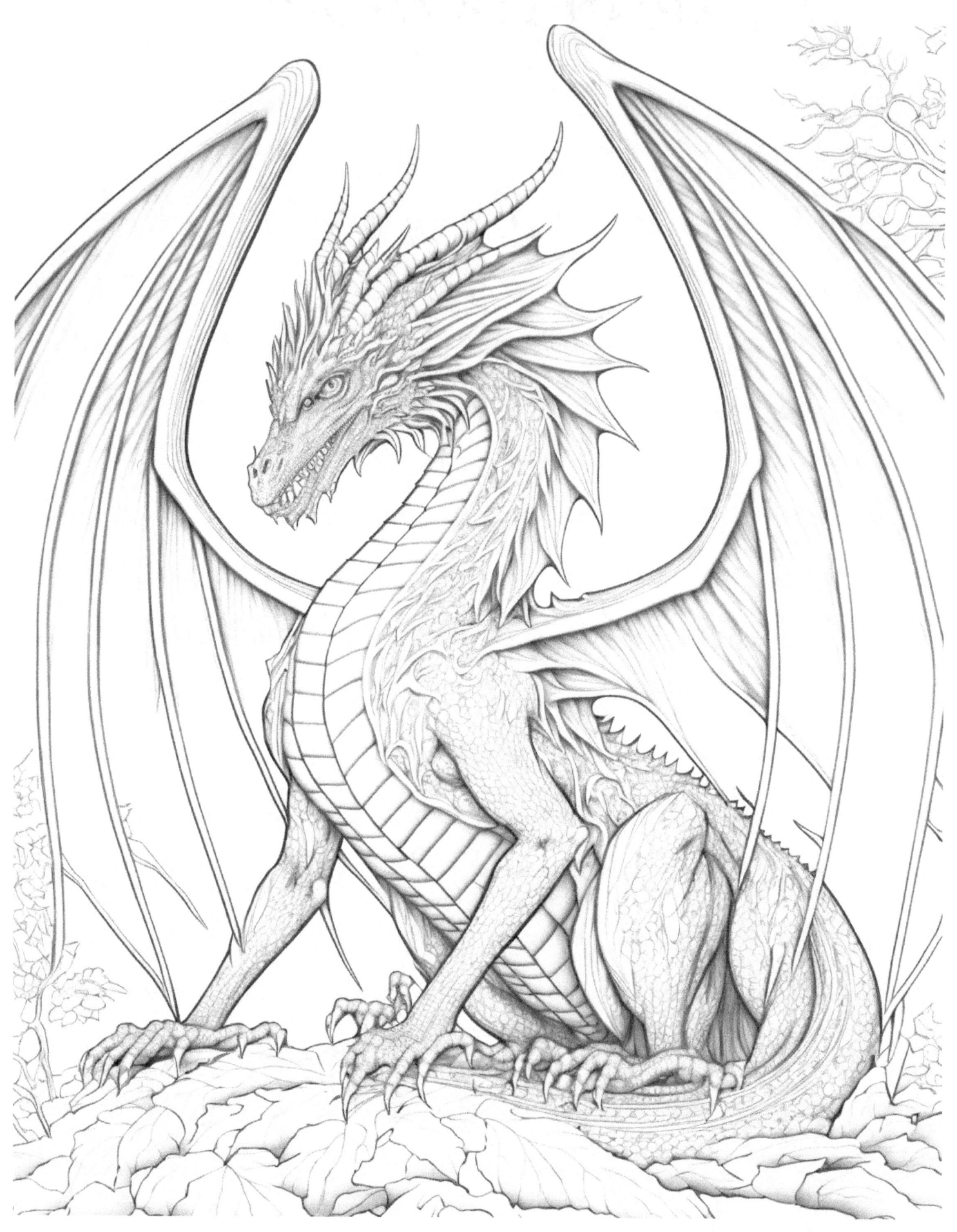

SPYING DRAGONS

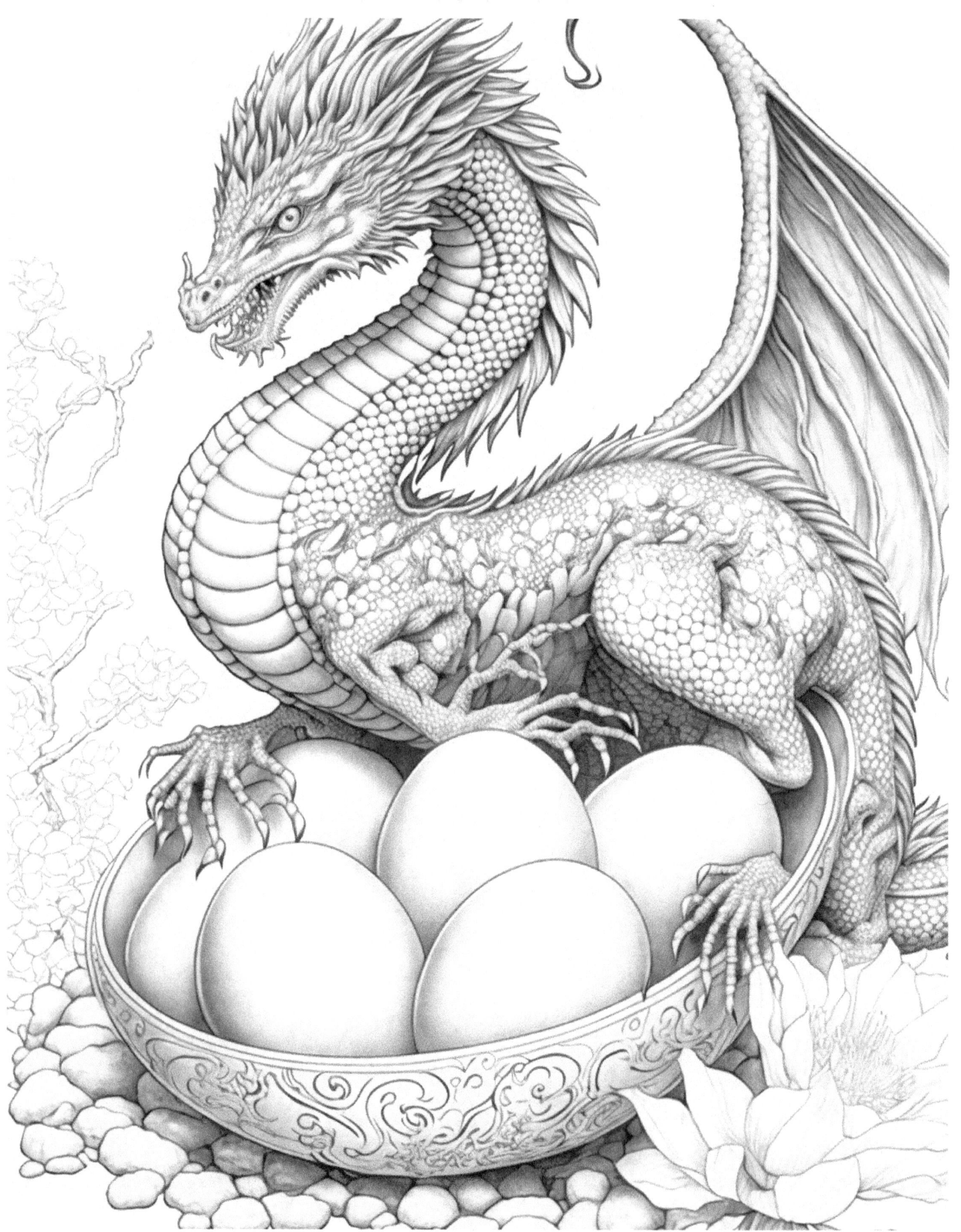

SPYING DRAGONS

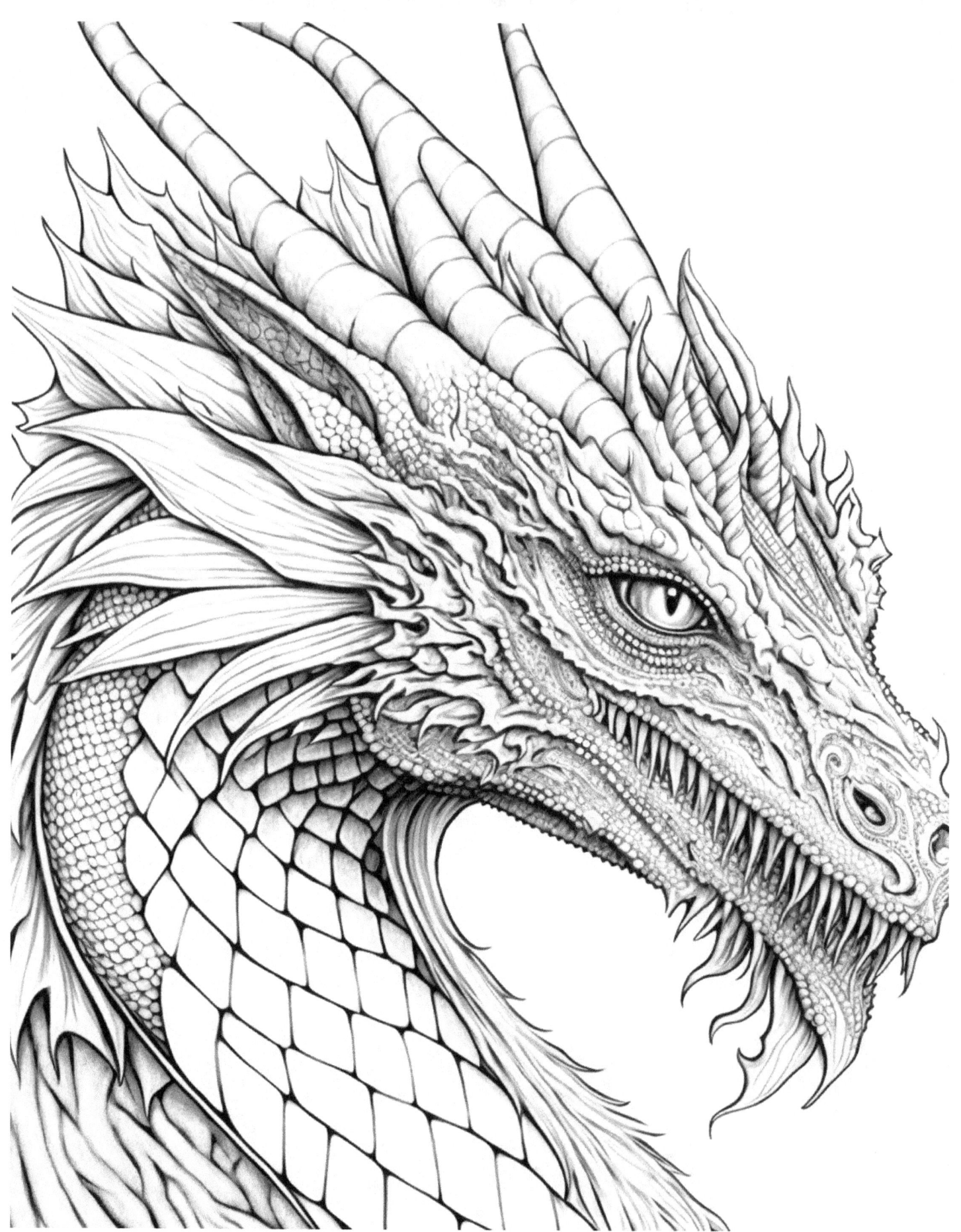

SPYING DRAGONS

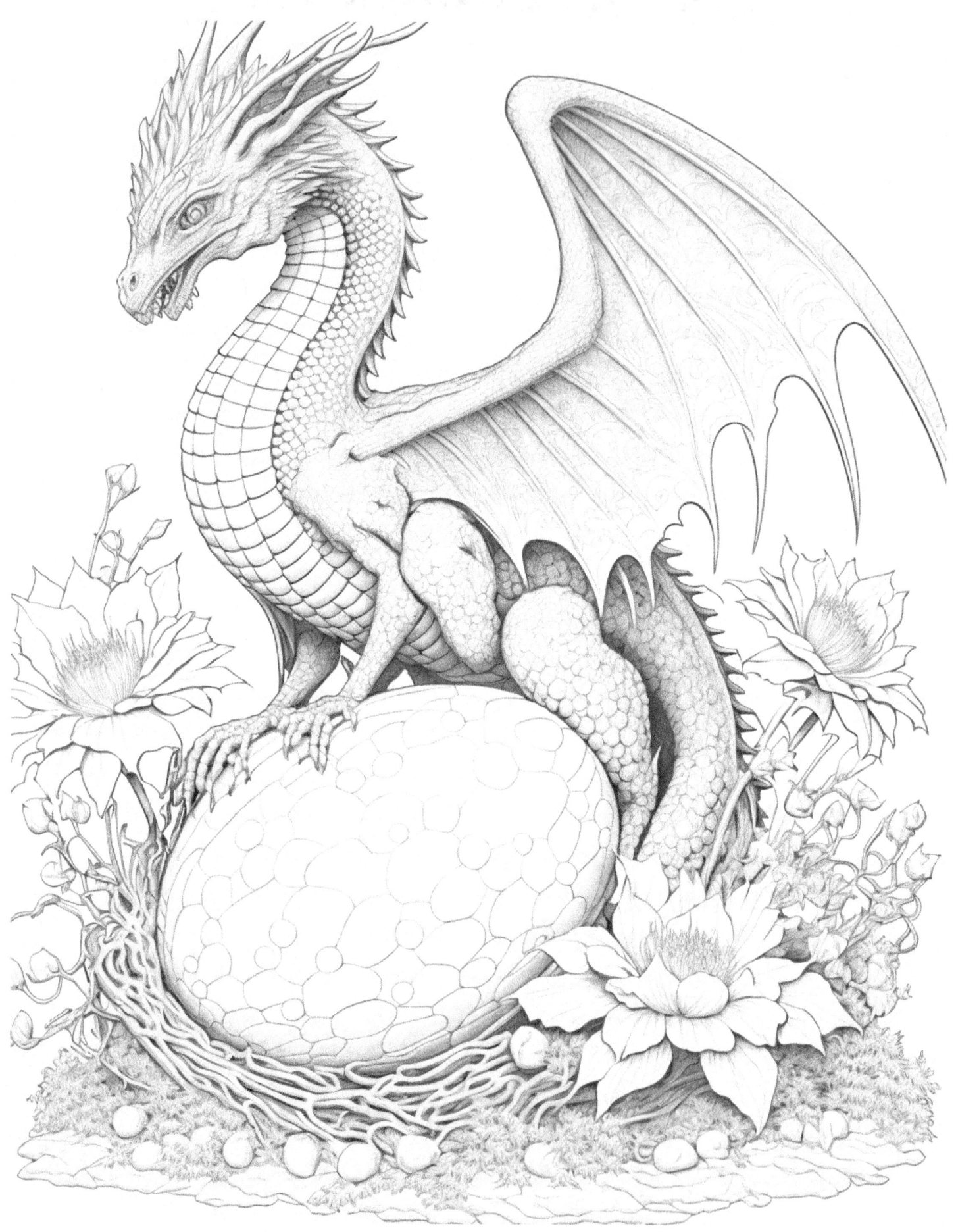

SPYING DRAGONS

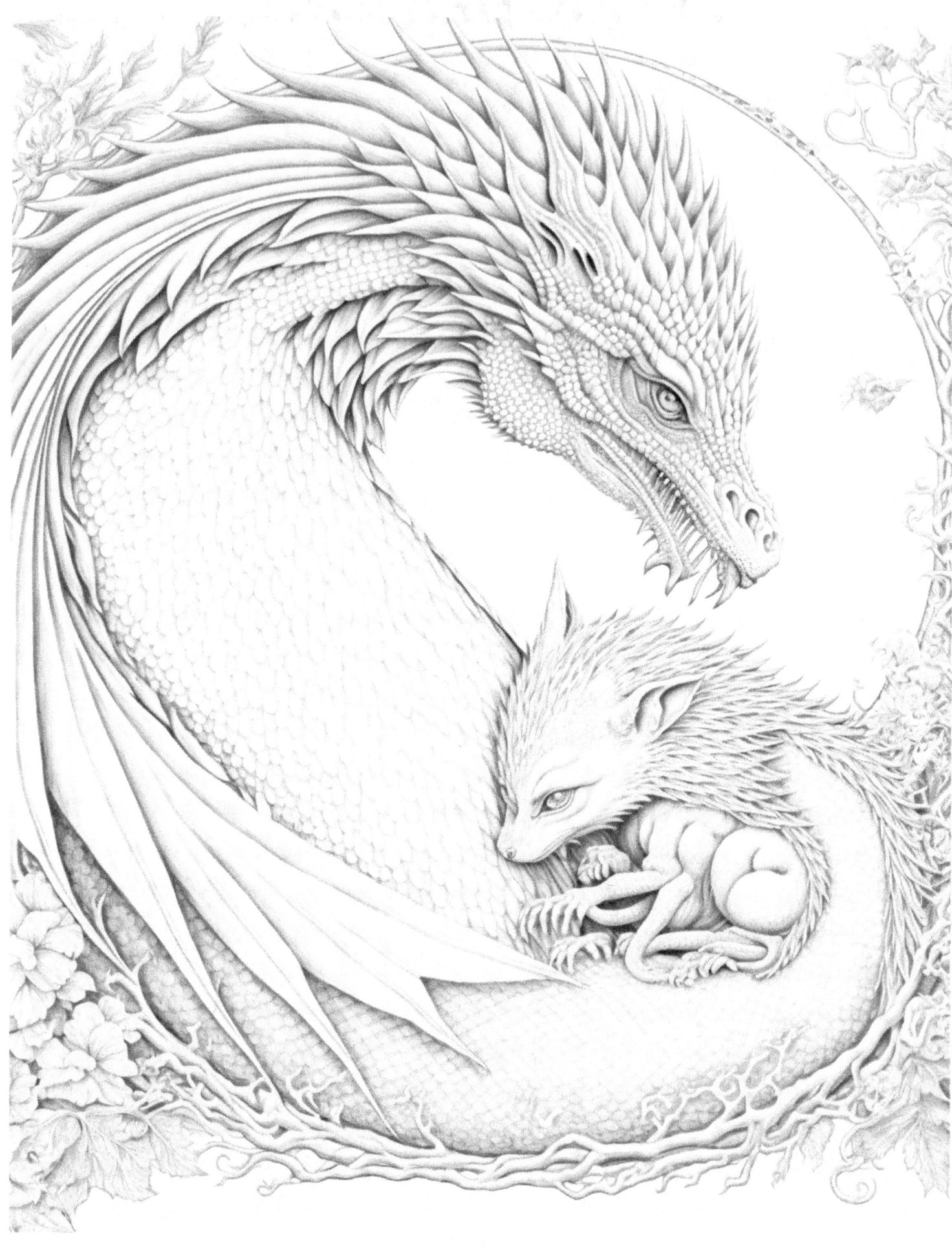

SPYING DRAGONS

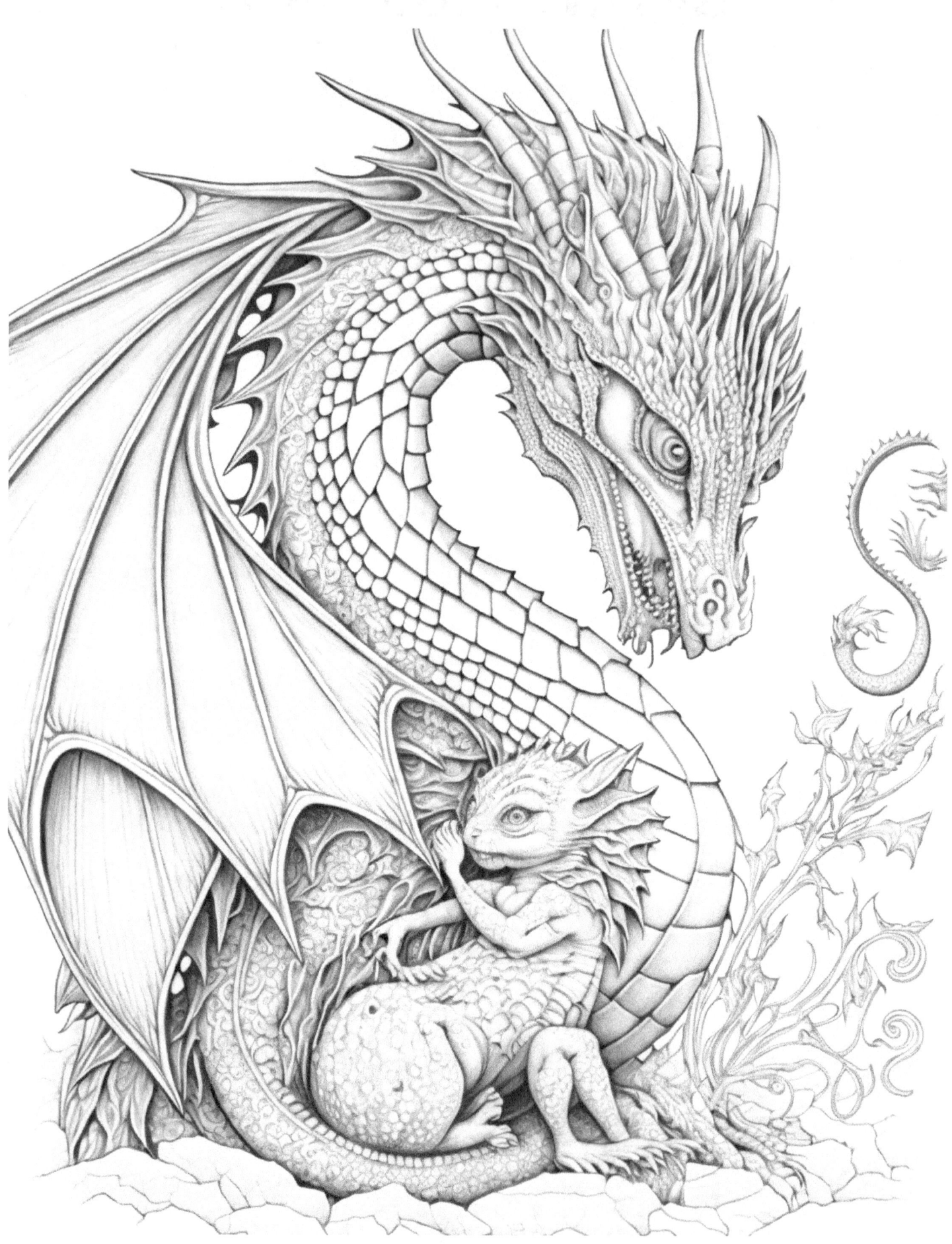

SPYING DRAGONS

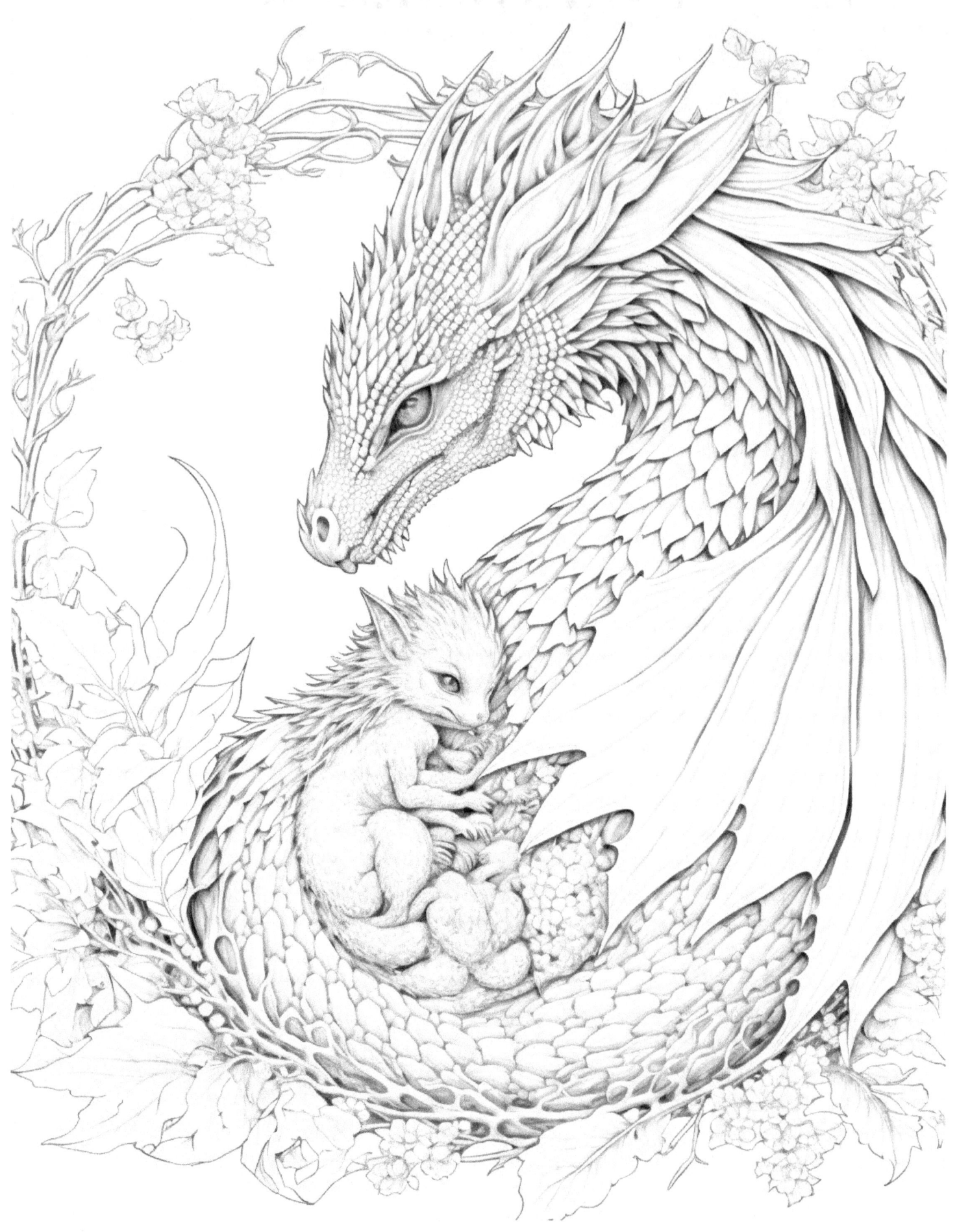

SPYING DRAGONS

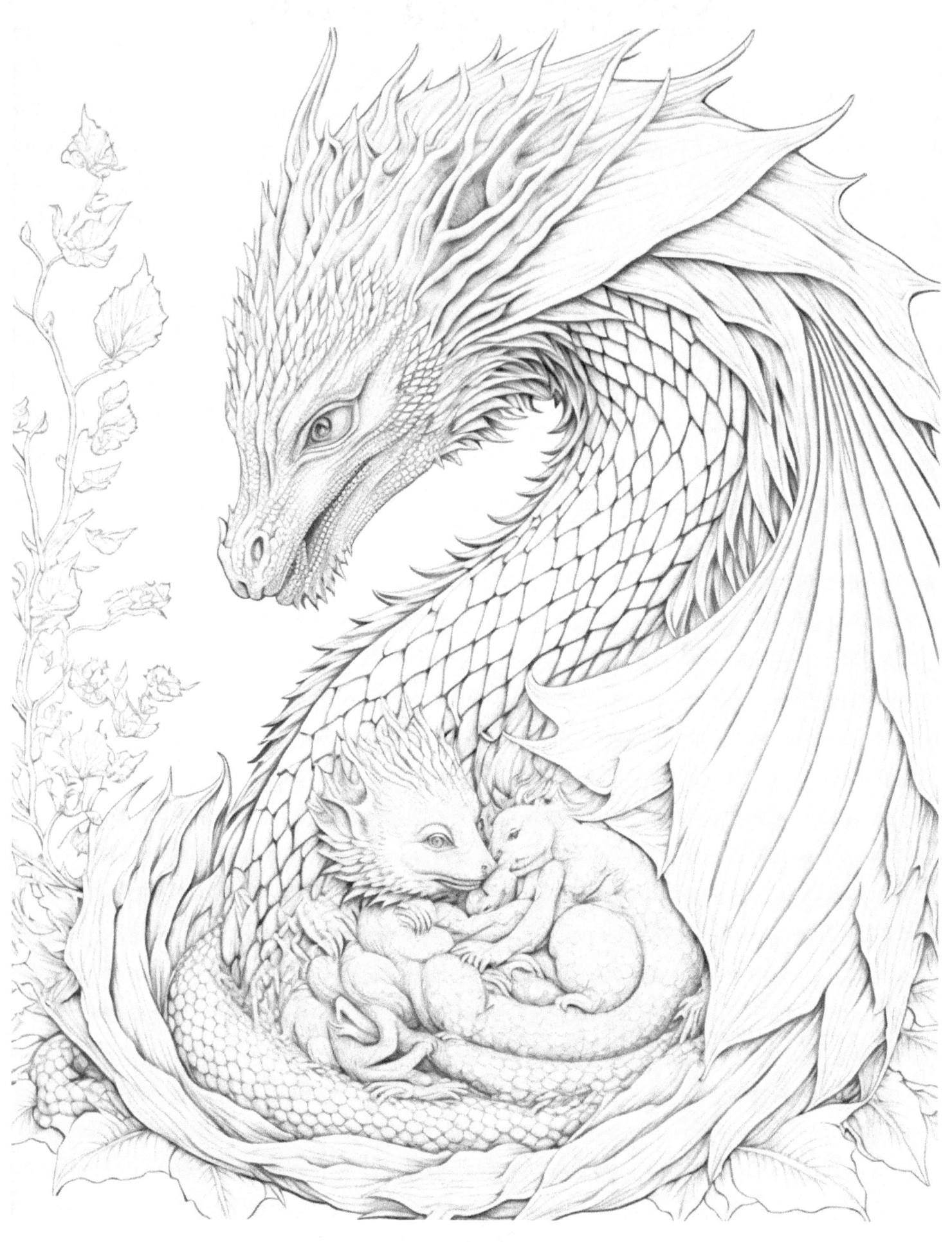

SPYING DRAGONS

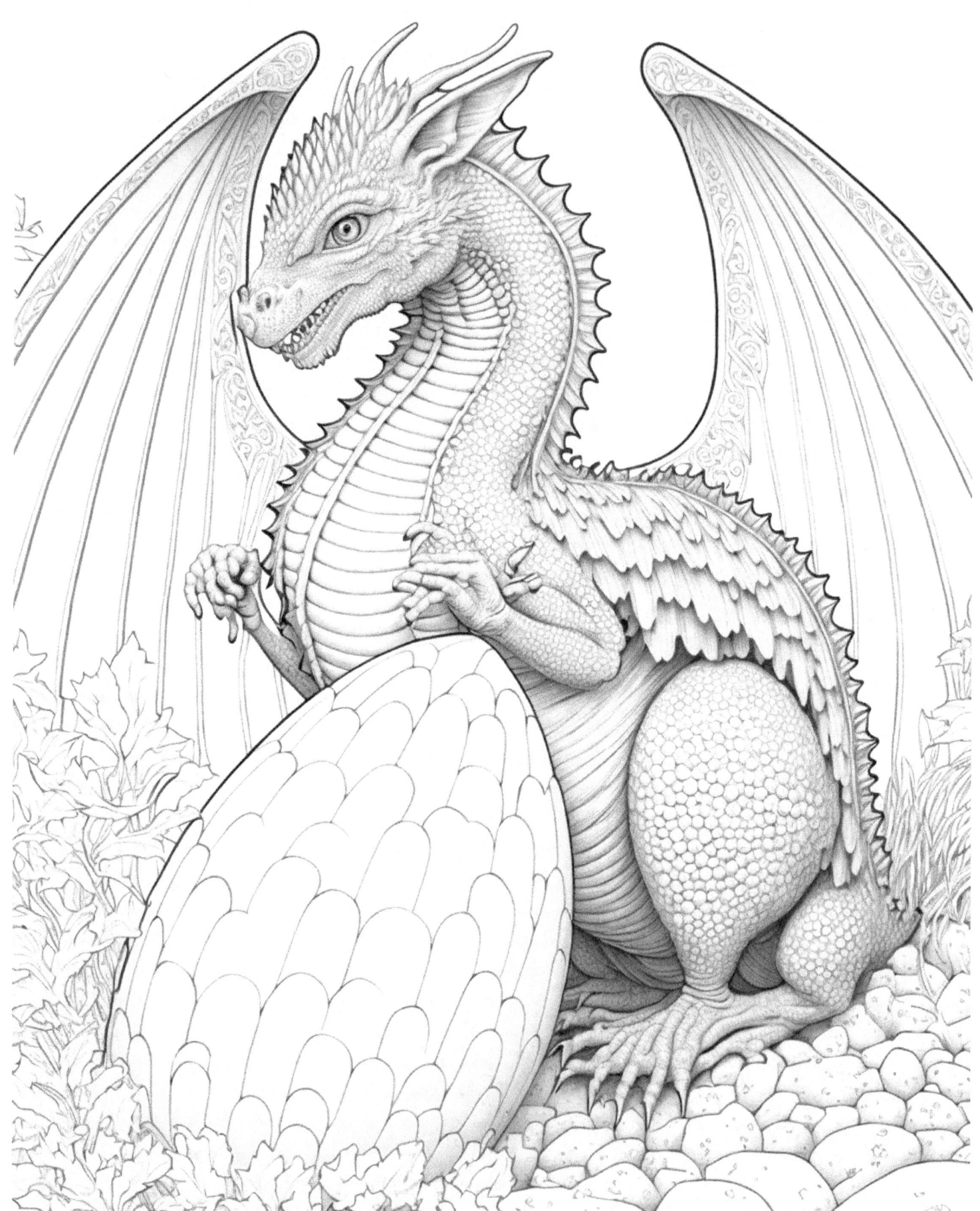

SPYING DRAGONS

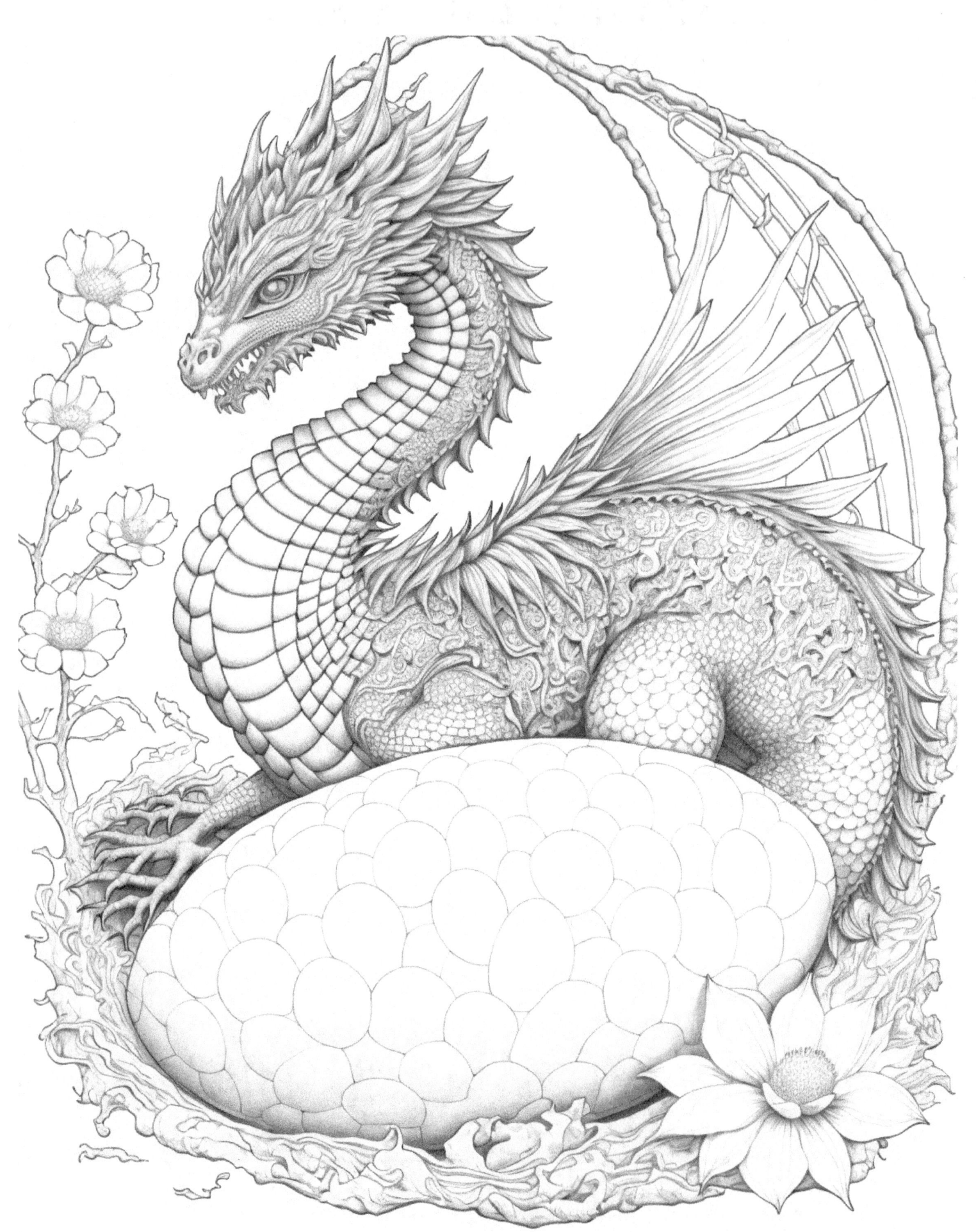

SPYING DRAGONS

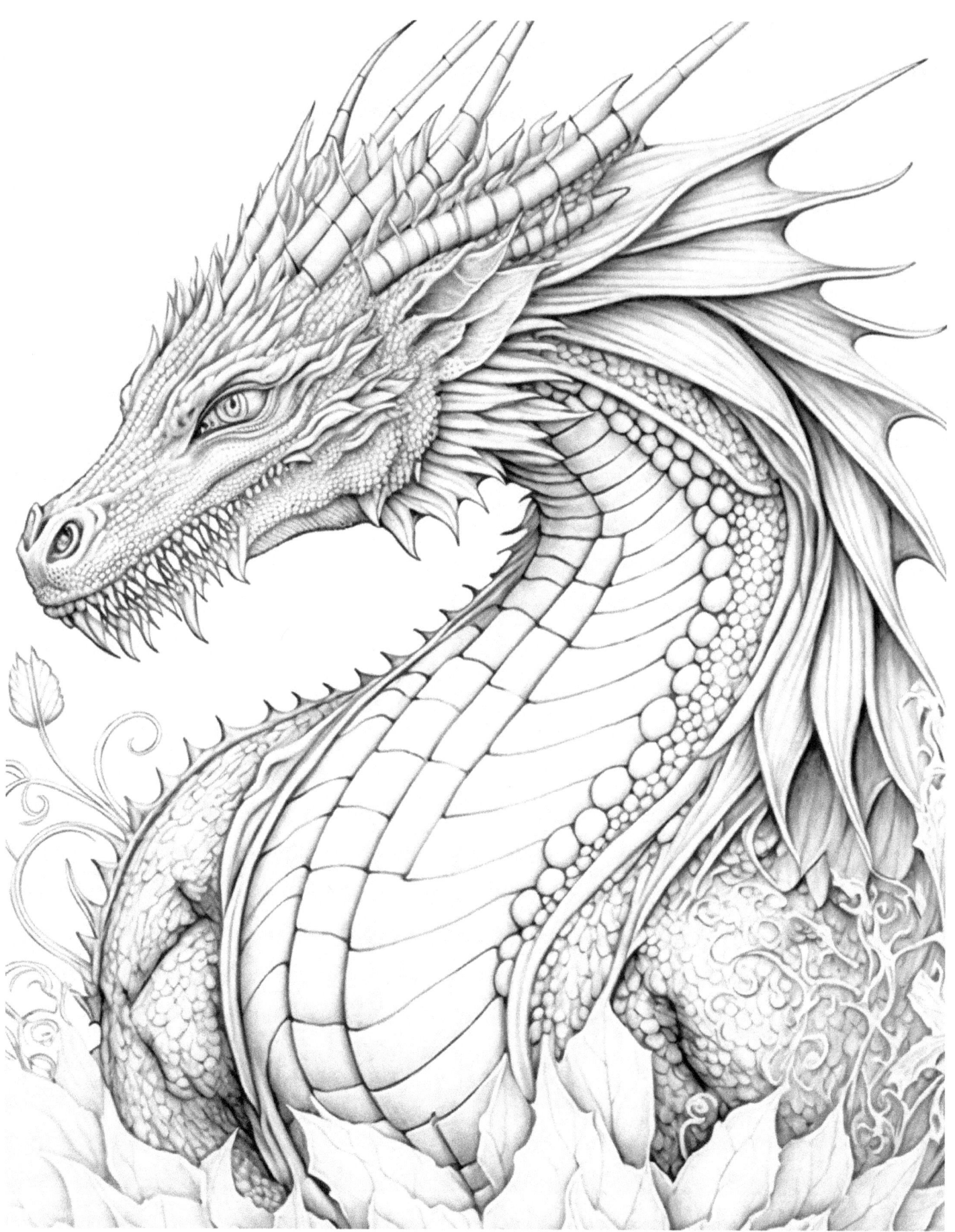

SPYING DRAGONS

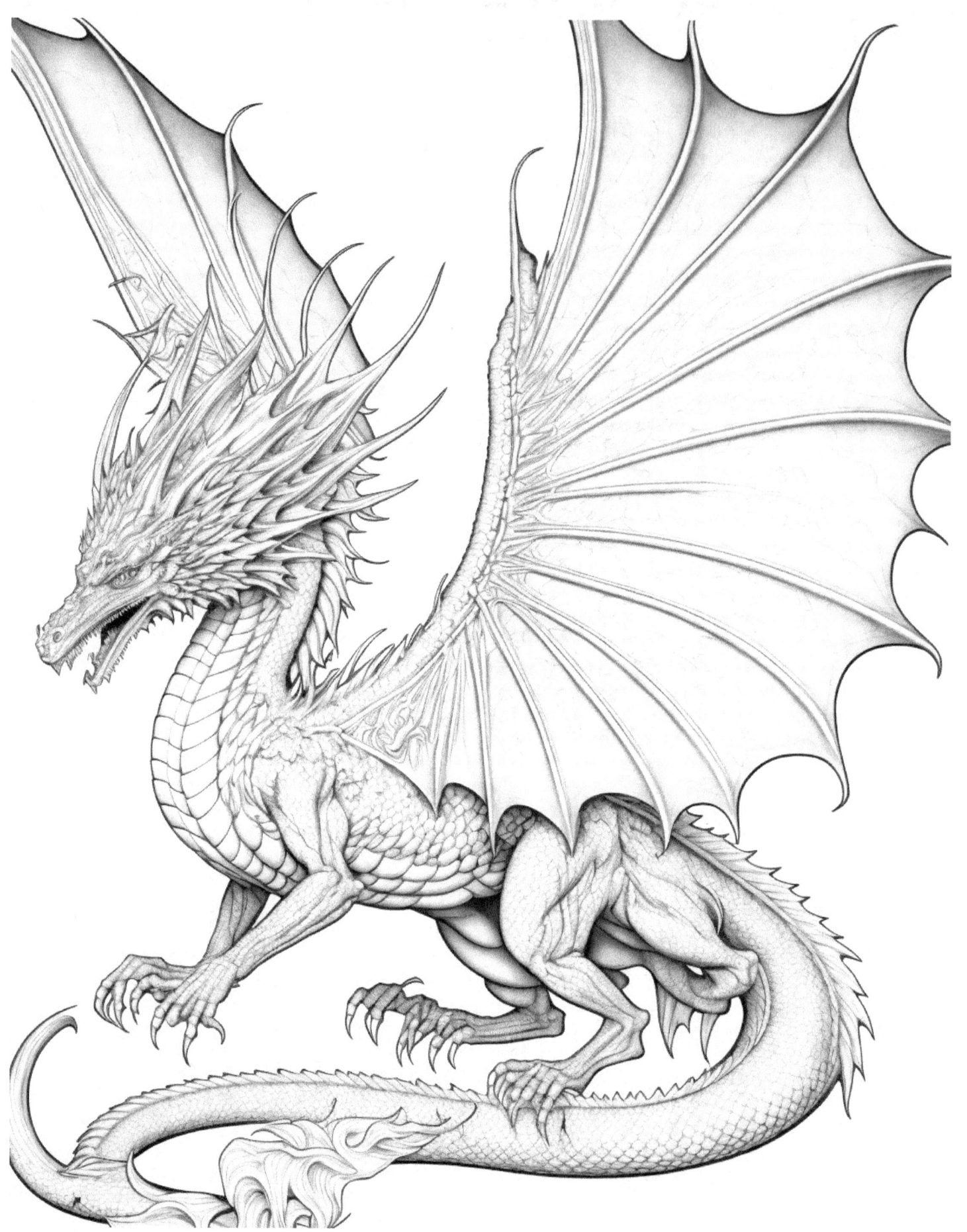

SPYING DRAGONS

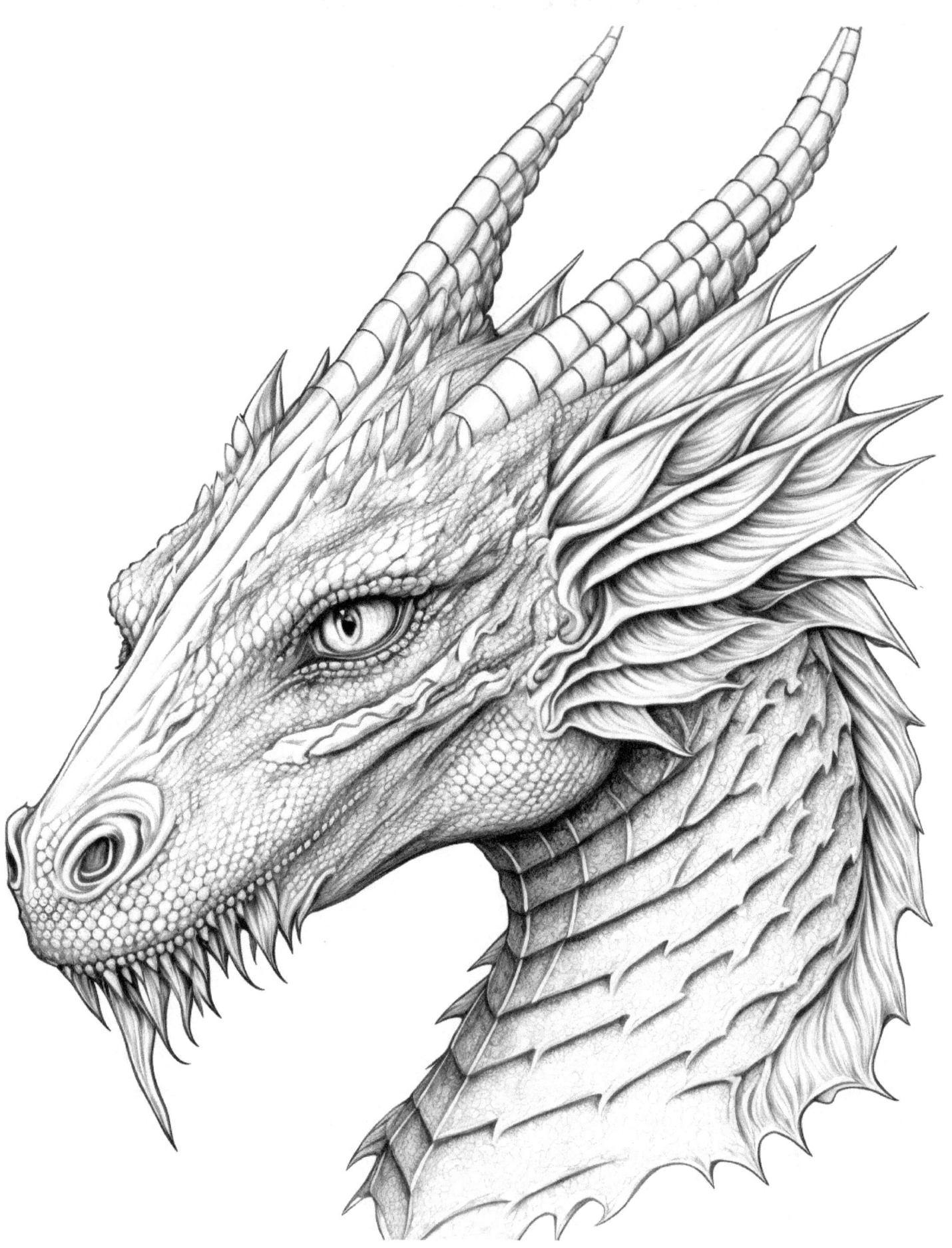

SPYING DRAGONS

www.ingramcontent.com/pod-product-compliance
Lightning Source LLC
Chambersburg PA
CBHW080947290526
45795CB00009B/2935

* 9 7 9 8 8 7 9 4 8 8 5 8 6 *